John Lennon's Message

from

Heaven

On the Spirit of Love and Peace, Music, and the Incredible Secret of His Soul

RYUHO OKAWA

HS PRESS

Contents

CHAPTER ONE

The Incredible Truth about John Lennon's Soul

John Lennon's Spiritual Message Part 1

1 Let the Rock Spirit Bring a Revolution to the Establishment

2 The Thought that John Lennon Put into His Music

CHAPTER TWO

The Power of Music
John Lennon's Spiritual Message Part 2

2   The Way of Thinking to Strengthen Your Influence

CHAPTER THREE

His Message to All the People
John Lennon's Spiritual Message Part 3

6 His Message to Everyone

7 Concluding Comments Regarding John Lennon's Astonishing Spiritual Message

Afterword 287

Preface

To be honest, the spiritual interview with John Lennon was also a shock to me. John was a man of the same era—he was still alive in my university days. At the time, I was buying cassette tapes of classical music conducted by Karajan in bulk, and was not so interested in the Beatles whose tapes were still piled up high on university cooperative although their popularity was already dying down. One of my friends told me, "You're a fool if you don't understand how great and genius the Beatles is." Forty years later, I was made to realize that fact.

I am not exactly sure what the difference is between Queen, who is now very popular with the movie *Bohemian Rhapsody*, and the Beatles.

Why is the soul of the main vocalist of Queen lost after death, while John Lennon, the main vocalist of the Beatles, is back in a higher-dimensional world in Heaven even though he was assassinated? There was something else in John besides purely rebellion against society, perhaps a noble spirit… But anyhow, I hope you will read through this book.

Ryuho Okawa
Master & CEO of Happy Science Group
February 1, 2019

CHAPTER ONE

The Incredible Truth about John Lennon's Soul

John Lennon's Spiritual Message Part 1

*Originally recorded in Japanese on January 14, 2019,
in the Special Lecture Hall of Happy Science in Japan,
and later translated into English.*

John Lennon (1940 - 1980)

John Lennon was a British rock singer who was born in Liverpool. After several changes to their band name, the Beatles was formed in 1960. He played a central role in the band and composed many of their songs and lyrics. In 1964, "I Want to Hold Your Hand" became hugely successful in the United States, exploding into a Beatles boom occurring across the globe. After their disbanding in 1970, John Lennon went to the United States and worked solo there. While mainly working there on his music, he continued giving many messages to the world, including those for the peace movement that he and his wife, Yoko Ono, both were involved in. He died in 1980 when he was shot by a crazed fan.

Interviewers from Happy Science[*]

Shio Okawa
Aide to Master & CEO

Yuki Wada
General Manager of the First Secretarial Division

General Manager of Overseas Missionary Work Promotion Office
   Religious Affairs Headquarters

The opinions of the spirit do not necessarily reflect those of Happy Science Group.
For the mechanism behind spiritual messages, see the end section.

[*] Interviewers are listed in the order that they appear in the transcript.
Their professional titles represent their positions at the time of the interview.

1

Let the Rock Spirit Bring a Revolution to the Establishment

His soul lives in the higher-dimensional world of Heaven

RYUHO OKAWA

Mr. John Lennon, Mr. John Lennon, could you come down? Mr. John Lennon, Mr. John Lennon, could you come down here? Mr. John Lennon, Mr. John Lennon...

[*Approximately ten seconds of silence pass.*]

JOHN LENNON

I'm John Lennon.

SHIO OKAWA
Are you able to speak in Japanese?

JOHN LENNON
Yes, I can.

SHIO OKAWA
Hello.

JOHN LENNON
Hello.

SHIO OKAWA
The guardian spirit of Mr. Paul McCartney came here several times.

JOHN LENNON
Yes, he's been helping to publicize about me.

SHIO OKAWA

Thank you for writing music with us before.*

JOHN LENNON

Any time an opportunity ever comes around, I'll help you again.

SHIO OKAWA

Are you living in Heaven?

JOHN LENNON

Yes, I am.

---

* John Lennon's spirit assisted in writing the original composition to "Lost Love," an insert song to the 2015 movie called, *The Laws of the Universe-Part 0*, and, "*Kimi no Maho ni Miserarete* [Enchanted by Your Magic]," an insert song to the 2019 movie called, *The Last White Witch*. Ryuho Okawa was the executive producer of both movies and he also authored their original stories.

SHIO OKAWA

Could we know what part of Heaven you are in?

JOHN LENNON

Well, the genre where I belong in might be different to yours, but you could say that my hotel room is on the same floor.

SHIO OKAWA

That's incredible! It must be because of the many people that you influenced.

JOHN LENNON

If there are religious leaders living on the other side of this floor, then towards my side there are artists.

SHIO OKAWA

I see, I see.

He is a branch spirit of Jesus Christ's soul and Paul McCartney is the rebirth of St. Paul

SHIO OKAWA
Are you able to talk with Jesus?

JOHN LENNON
Yes.

SHIO OKAWA
That's incredible!

WADA
Are you an old friend or acquaintance of his?

JOHN LENNON
Yes.

SHIO OKAWA
What is your connection with him?

JOHN LENNON

Hmmm. I am probably a branch spirit of his soul.

WADA

You're a branch spirit of his soul!?

SHIO OKAWA

Are you really!?

JOHN LENNON

Yes. Hasn't McCartney (his guardian spirit)[*] said before that he is St. Paul?

SHIO OKAWA

He has told us that, yes.

WADA

Is that also true?

---

[*] Before the spiritual message from John Lennon in this chapter was taken, a spiritual message from Paul McCartney's guardian spirit was also recorded. Paul McCartney's guardian spirit revealed in it that he was St. Paul in a past life.

JOHN LENNON

Yes, it's true.

WADA

That's incredible!

SHIO OKAWA

You were here many times because of that, is that true?

JOHN LENNON

Yes, it means that I am one of your religious friends. And when guidance from Jesus was given to you, it was received in his name.

Now is the age of influence, and replicating traditional religions is not enough

SHIO OKAWA

Is Mr. Tolstoy* also in your soul group?

JOHN LENNON

He's one of us, yes.

SHIO OKAWA

You've been to the field of literature and also the field of music, then...

JOHN LENNON

The fields of literature and music... I heard that Zeus† also went to the field of movies. His heroes

---

* The literary giant of Russia, Leo Tolstoy, was also a part of Jesus Christs' soul. See "A Spiritual Message from Tolstoy" held on August 24, 2012. This video and all the following spiritual messages can be watched at the Happy Science temples around the world.

† It was revealed in a spiritual message from the guardian spirit of Stan Lee, the creator of the Avengers and an American comic book writer, that he is a part of Zeus' soul. This video is called, "Spiritual Interview with the Guardian Spirit of Stan Lee 'The Space Age and Heroes,'" held on September 22, 2018.

are being brought into creation through the world of movies, so these times we live in now are different. We are no longer living in ancient times.

SHIO OKAWA
Will Ms. Yoko Ono be returning to Heaven?

JOHN LENNON
(In her past life), her name was Maria, Malta, or one of those kinds of names. There were many women (around Jesus) with those names.

SHIO OKAWA
There were many women named Maria, I see.

JOHN LENNON
You see, the times have changed now. Now is the age of influence, and replicating old-fashioned religions is not enough.

SHIO OKAWA

You must be giving your assistance to El Cantare, then.

JOHN LENNON

I've felt the need to do so, but I've also been expounding the teachings. For a very long time, I've continuously preached teachings on love. Only, they've been coming from the core consciousness of Jesus Christ, and we, others, have been giving assistance in literature and the arts. But you've also been creating songs with Jesus, haven't you?

SHIO OKAWA

Yes, we have.

JOHN LENNON

Hahahahaha [*laughs*]. He wrote the pep song for the Happy Science Academy, for example. He also wrote the songs and lyrics to *Heart to Heart** and *Life Is Beautiful*†. Although, well, it's kind of a funny thing.

During his life on Earth, Jesus "rocked" the established religion

SHIO OKAWA

The long hairstyle that you wore later on in your life (on Earth) was a little similar to Jesus Christ's [*laughs*].

JOHN LENNON

If I say this, all of rock 'n' roll will become Christianity and the Vatican will be against that, so I need to avoid doing that, but Jesus

---

* "Heart to Heart" is the title of the theme song to the documentary entitled, *Heart to Heart*. Released in May 2018, this film's original concept was authored by Ryuho Okawa.

† "Life Is Beautiful" is the title of the theme song to the documentary entitled, *Life Is Beautiful*. Released in 2019, this film's original concept was authored by Ryuho Okawa.

was actually a "rock" person. His time was an age of "rock."

SHIO OKAWA
He transcended the norms, that is true.

JOHN LENNON
So, back then, the religion of Judaism was the equivalent of what the Vatican is today. So he was "rocking" the established religion of his time. He was "singing" and "rocking" his own times.

SHIO OKAWA
Wow, panda's* excited.

JOHN LENNON
Panda's excited?

SHIO OKAWA
You're incredible, Mr. John Lennon.

---

* Sometimes, Aide to Master and CEO, Shio Okawa, calls herself "panda."

The modern love-and-peace movement in music is taking the place of Christianity

JOHN LENNON

You can be friends with Yoko Ono.

SHIO OKAWA

Really? I'm happy to hear that.

JOHN LENNON

Yes, you'd be able to.

WADA

Did the two other members (of the Beatles, George Harrison and Ringo Starr,) also have any relation with Christianity...?

JOHN LENNON

Well, I can't say anything unless they say so

themselves, since it's their right to reveal that about themselves. But who knows? They could have been one of the twelve apostles. Hahahaha [*laughs*].

The love and peace movement in modern music activism, environmental activism, and the anti-war movement may be taking on the role of Christianity because the Vatican has become powerless.

SHIO OKAWA
Mr. Lennon, you are speaking in Japanese so fluently.

JOHN LENNON
Yes, I can speak it very well, it's true. Maybe you wanted me to speak in English, or maybe in Panda English? In Panglish? But I can speak fluent Japanese.

Jesus disregarded established powers and authorities

JOHN LENNON

You've uncovered the secret that I am (a branch spirit of) Jesus' soul. Recently, (Jesus' soul) has been very diligent. He has also appeared as Tolstoy.

SHIO OKAWA

Mr. McCartney (his guardian spirit) comes often but you do not appear so much at least by the name of John Lennon. So I was wondering what kind of person you are.

JOHN LENNON

Well, I have been doing a lot of your work. (Jesus has been) making many songs for you, so I was hoping you'll notice something that's strange about that.

SHIO OKAWA

I see, the song "Lost Love" you made was a nice song.

JOHN LENNON

I make the songs in Jesus' name.

WADA

I see. That's right.

JOHN LENNON

Here, Jesus sings songs, right? It's puzzling. The Christians will be surprised if they hear this.

SHIO OKAWA

That's true. Jesus' soul has quite a variety.

JOHN LENNON

Yeah, he has an artistic side. But he's also a rocker. His way of life is a rocker. Or you could say that he was kind of like an American hippie.

SHIO OKAWA

Yes, he is a rocker.

JOHN LENNON

He gathered disciples who were fishermen, tax collectors, and a prostitute. He's really rock 'n' roll. He completely ignores established powers and authorities.

SHIO OKAWA

And norms and social statuses... He removes all of that.

JOHN LENNON

Right, right. Yeah, so if I weren't John Lennon, I'd want to say I'm Steve Jobs of Apple. They're all rockers.

SHIO OKAWA

I understand.

JOHN LENNON

The times are different now. You shouldn't be confined to old ways of thinking. Now is the age of influence. So the question is what influential power you will have.

The Beatles and Queen are both rock bands, but there's a difference between them

JOHN LENNON
So, the other day...

SHIO OKAWA
Queen.*

JOHN LENNON
Zoroaster said that (80 to 90 percent of) rock 'n'

---

* A spiritual message from Freddie Mercury, the vocalist of the British rock band, Queen, was held on January 12, 2019. See "The Spiritual Messages from Freddie Mercury and Zoroaster."

roll music is hellish. But this is not necessarily true of all rock music.

SHIO OKAWA
Well that is wrong, probably.

JOHN LENNON
It's different music.

SHIO OKAWA
Beatles' songs are different. It's not disturbing, even if it's rock.

WADA
They have different vibrations.

JOHN LENNON
Right.

WADA
They're relaxing.

JOHN LENNON

There's purity. Usually, there's a stronger trend to do music that's like rock in Hell because heavenly music is boring.

SHIO OKAWA

That's true. Like the movie, *Too Young To Die! Wakakushite Shinu**.

JOHN LENNON

Yes, yes.

WADA

Yeah, that's true. It's rackety.

JOHN LENNON

Yes, that's right.

---

* The name of a Japanese movie released in 2016. *Too Young To Die! Wakakushite Shinu*, directed by Kankuro Kudo (2016; Japan: Toho Company Ltd., Asmik Ace, Inc., 2016), DVD.

In recent times, ninth-dimensional spirits are being reborn more often to nourish this world

JOHN LENNON

Well, so, I'm a branch spirit (of Jesus), but recently, the age is transforming rapidly. We, the ninth-dimensional spirits, are being reborn more frequently and nourishing this world. Frequently. Very frequently.

WADA

Are there others? Other branch spirits on Earth?

JOHN LENNON

Well, yeah, ninth-dimensional spirits are being reborn to this world and appearing in various fields. So, as I said before, there could be someone in the industrial field. Maybe. It's that kind of age now. I don't know, in terms of influence, don't large corporations have a global scale? It transcends nations, so the ninth-dimensional spirits could be reborn in these other places. You will need to spiritually research this more thoroughly. You may have to. Yes.

SHIO OKAWA

So, maybe Steve Jobs could also be…

JOHN LENNON

And maybe GAFA. Google, Apple, Facebook, Amazon, and maybe others such as Microsoft or maybe some in Japan. You may want to do a guardian spirit reading of Carlos Ghosn, too.

WADA

Person of the time.

JOHN LENNON

What if he's the only Angel of Light born to France? No, no, Lebanon. There's no one else greater than him in Lebanon. You need to be a bit more diligent.

The spiritual reason that led to conflict with the Vatican

SHIO OKAWA
John, you are from which star? Which planet?

JOHN LENNON
Planet? Hmm… Well there's Jesus' planet, so…

SHIO OKAWA
Oh, Sagittarius?

JOHN LENNON
I need to make it the same as Jesus' planet. But in reality, well, I'm doing a "concert tour" so, I'm sowing seeds in many places, of course.

SHIO OKAWA
Mr. Metatron* came the other day.

JOHN LENNON

Hmm, there's Metatron, too. That name sounds like if he is born today, he'd be so huge.

SHIO OKAWA

Huge?

JOHN LENNON

From the name.

SHIO OKAWA

Ahh. I see, the "meta" part [*laughs*].

JOHN LENNON

Hmm. I think he'd be huge, probably. I think so. Hmm, like the guy in *Ghostbusters*. Like the Marshmallow Man.

---

* Metatron is a space being from Planet Include, the home planet of Jesus Christ's cosmic soul, which is located in the Sagittarius constellation. He appeared in the UFO reading taken on January 1, 2019, entitled, "UFO Reading: 2019 New Year Address, Prophecy Edition from the Planet of Love."

WADA

I see.

JOHN LENNON

So, John Lennon is one part of Jesus Christ.

SHIO OKAWA

Wow, this is a scoop we got even before doing a spiritual message (for release)!

JOHN LENNON

That's right. Hmm, so, it's only natural that I'd get in a conflict with the Vatican. It has been said that if Jesus was reborn, the Vatican would definitely persecute him. Dostoevsky made predictions of that, too. The church doesn't need Jesus. It just troubles them.

SHIO OKAWA

Jesus himself doesn't like the atmosphere of the church either, right?

JOHN LENNON

Well the bureaucracy of the church, in Dostoevsky's words, would be that they're taken over by Devils. They're doing things to protect their interests. So, they're the same as being a king. The Devils are able to enter them, so I think Jesus won't like that.

Rock music can destroy communist systems

JOHN LENNON

Rock 'n' roll will shake the authority of the church. Well, Luther* is also a rocker, too. At least in a sense, in that age. He fought against the church in that era.

---

* Martin Luther was the originator of German religious reform. He believed the Bible should be the sole fountainhead of Christianity, and wrote the Ninety-Five Theses, his propositions against the Catholic Pope's distribution of indulgences. He greatly affected the Catholic church, and influenced the forming of the Protestant church. He also translated the Bible into German and contributed greatly to forming the modern German language.

SHIO OKAWA

The aim of your rock spirit is important.

JOHN LENNON

In China too, many are being born for the revolution. There are many people being born. So, even if it is unexpected, you should judge people by how much influence he or she is exhibiting.

SHIO OKAWA

Well, yes but Mao Zedong went rock in the other direction so…

JOHN LENNON

That's true. His influence was huge, it's true. But if it gets to that scale, you could consider possible influence from the flip-side of the universe[*]. If

---

[*] See "A Spiritual Interview with Mao Zedong" held on November 15, 2018.

you rock 'n' roll in China all the way, it'll break the Establishment.

SHIO OKAWA

I see. It's true that rock songs sing about personal freedom.

JOHN LENNON

If rock becomes popular, and music and movies become freely distributed, Mao Zedong's and Xi Jinping's establishment would collapse. Stan Lee's American heroes are actually destroying China and communism. That's what it is.

SHIO OKAWA

Panda's excited.

JOHN LENNON

Is panda excited? I've got to save the pandas from Sichuan... What if the pandas of Sichuan do a panda rock 'n' roll? If the pandas started to sing?

SHIO OKAWA

[*Singing*] Panda♪ Love and freedom and faith~♪ Democracy~♪

JOHN LENNON

Ryoma Sakamoto* could say he was a panda in a past life.

SHIO OKAWA

Well, with Ryoma it could be possible.

"We were trying to change the world."

JOHN LENNON

So, the Beatles sold several hundred million albums and became a worldwide...

---

* In a previous spiritual reading, Aide to Master and CEO, Shio Okawa, was revealed as having been Ryoma Sakamoto in her past life. She has authored *Panda-Gaku Nyumon* [An Introduction to Panda-ism: My Way of Life and Thinking], and the *Panda Roonda* children's books series, all published by IRH Press.

SHIO OKAWA

Someone said that it sold over a billion albums throughout the world...

JOHN LENNON

Many people were paying attention to whether we surpassed Jesus or not,* and we faced oppression and it probably led to my assassination, I believe. So, that's how we were trying to change the world.

SHIO OKAWA

Wow.

JOHN LENNON

That's what happens to things that grow on a global scale. So, Happy Science is currently in need of such power. A population of little over

---

* In 1966, when John Lennon remarked about being "more popular than Jesus," and said that "Jesus was all right, but his disciples were thick and ordinary," he raised controversy in the United States and other Christian countries.

one hundred million is trying to seal you, Happy Science, as just one of the Japanese religions. You should not be sealed. You've got to grow like the Beatles.

SHIO OKAWA

You had a huge influence on the world. Rock 'n' rollers and revolutionaries get clearly divided in terms of those going to Heaven or to Hell.

Happy Science and Shakyamuni Buddha are also "rockers" in some meaning

JOHN LENNON

You, too, are trying to destroy the system of North Korea, China, and Thailand, right? So, you're doing rock.

SHIO OKAWA

That's true, maybe. Master gave a lecture for Thai people and in it, he said that each person has

Buddha-nature within.* That part may be sung as a rock song.

JOHN LENNON
Shyakyamuni Buddha is rock, too, in a sense. He renounced his status as a prince, left his wife and son, and freely went into self-discipline.

SHIO OKAWA
True!

WADA
That's a new definition.

JOHN LENNON
That's rock.

SHIO OKAWA
He went on throwing away the status structure that existed for so long. He removed it.

---

* See chapter two, "What Is 'Truth'?" in Ryuho Okawa, *The Age of Mercy* (Tokyo: HS Press, 2019).

JOHN LENNON

See, well, he didn't directly address it, but his philosophy went against the caste system. So, he did destroy the status structure. So, the lower-class people of India seem to be attracted to Buddhism because it destroys that. We aren't divided by whether or not we want the established systems to continue. Confucius looked like he was maintaining the existing system but people of that age actually could not accept his teachings. In that age (that he lived in)...

"Happy Science is also in need of a new rock 'n' roll spirit"

JOHN LENNON

Hm. These people are actually being born more often and doing various work but they aren't regarded that highly, so they're keeping quiet.

SHIO OKAWA

When you think of this, I feel the gods are filled with love. They are being born more frequently and working.

JOHN LENNON

If you said that John Lennon was Jesus Christ, many Christians would get angry, and people who like rock 'n' roll might get persecuted. So we need to be careful. Um, my words, "Jesus was all right, but his disciples were thick and ordinary," were my honest feeling.

SHIO OKAWA

That's true.

JOHN LENNON

They were pretty pathetic—the twelve disciples. They all escaped and betrayed me. That cannot be forgiven. It makes me want to do rock, truly. That's why I used music this time to destroy the world. Songs would unknowingly convey everything. So, you are making movies now but you should develop some new tools. If you are too attached to the fact that you are religious professionals, things won't go that well.

SHIO OKAWA

Well, in Master's case, he is the one that created various fields of study. He is the source of everything so it's true that he cannot be categorized under the current definition of religion.

JOHN LENNON

So you're calling UFOs now and speaking to space beings.* You're starting to do rock. Hmm. You're the spokespeople for these space beings.

SHIO OKAWA

That's true. We're not talking about whether UFOs exist or not, we're already talking with them.

JOHN LENNON

Yes, that's rock. This is like new brainwashing. Our mere songs were able to reach the world. You've got to do a new rock 'n' roll, or else, it won't reach people. In Japan you may have published a lot in terms of number, but they're not selling explosively.

---

* See Ryuho Okawa, *UFOs Caught on Camera!: A Spiritual Investigation on Videos and Photos of the Luminous Objects Visiting Earth* (Tokyo: HS Press, 2018).

What John Lennon's work
in Heaven is right now

SHIO OKAWA

Mr. John Lennon, what is your work in Heaven, now?

JOHN LENNON

Well, I guess I'm supporting you mainly in artistic things.

SHIO OKAWA

I see. Thank you very much.

JOHN LENNON

Well, I'm kind of hoping that you will open the path to new work for me. I'm expecting a lot from you.

WADA

Thank you.

SHIO OKAWA

Then, you would support us even more?

JOHN LENNON

Well, the other day a messiah of music, Lord Heem*, appeared. So, it's easier for me to come out and appear now.

SHIO OKAWA

You're related to Lord Heem too…

JOHN LENNON

Well, um, I shouldn't talk so definitively.

SHIO OKAWA

Panda's excited.

---

* See the spiritual message held on November 12, 2018, entitled, "A Spiritual Message from the Central God of Vega, Heem."

JOHN LENNON

If Ms. Sayaka's song or Ms. Sengen's song could become a hit, no one would have a problem with that. It can be in any way, you just have to deliver a great result. You have to become greater, like get over one hundred million downloads like a certain someone. Otherwise Happy Science won't spread. But you're fixated on being small. So again, it's a lack of power on the disciples' part.

SHIO OKAWA

We're living in a miraculous age when the Creator is on Earth.

JOHN LENNON

Right. So, the disciples need to work harder.

SHIO OKAWA

I'm sorry about that.

JOHN LENNON

Even we were able to make ourselves international, so you need more of that kind of power, too. That's what I'm saying. Excited?

SHIO OKAWA

Panda is excited.

JOHN LENNON

How about you sing?

SHIO OKAWA

No, I'm a terrible singer...

JOHN LENNON

How about a fight choreography then? Be a stage combat movie star!

SHIO OKAWA

[*Laughs*] That's a tall order...

JOHN LENNON
Appear as a female sword-wielding warrior.

SHIO OKAWA
[*Laughs*] I don't think so. I'm sorry. Thank you, though.

China's personality shows in their use of "panda diplomacy"

JOHN LENNON
Well, if you consider yourself a panda, you're a great threat to the Chinese government.

SHIO OKAWA
Pandas do not belong solely to China.

JOHN LENNON
You can lead the campaign for not returning Xiang Xiang, the panda, to China.

SHIO OKAWA

That's "rock." Rock 'n' roll. Xiang Xiang was born and raised in Japan after all. We should make a song called, "We Love Xiang Xiang."

WADA

Well in a way, the pandas are hostages, aren't they.

JOHN LENNON

That's right.

WADA

China's…

JOHN LENNON

The panda's cubs are diplomats that they'll withdraw when they don't like something.

SHIO OKAWA

Xiang Xiang is loved so much because she earns a lot of money.

JOHN LENNON

Well, it's a "great" country.

SHIO OKAWA

It reflects their character as a country, doesn't it?

JOHN LENNON

There you have it.

SHIO OKAWA

Thank you.

Wishing for Happy Science overseas to make a breakthrough and become widely known throughout the world

JOHN LENNON

A long time went by before you actually looked into me after you were asked to do so. You aren't as assiduous as you say.

SHIO OKAWA

I'm sorry about that. Mr. McCartney's guardian spirit came three times to speak to us.

JOHN LENNON

Then next time, you should go to Hollywood and sing there.

SHIO OKAWA

Some people from around Hollywood said that the song* was great, that they loved it.

JOHN LENNON

Right! So sing! Haha [*laughs*]. It'll be great. I would love to see that happen.

WADA

We want to do our best.

---

* Shio Okawa is referring to a song from the 2018 movie, *The Laws of the Universe-Part I*, for which Ryuho Okawa was executive producer. He also authored the original story of the movie.

JOHN LENNON

It would be great to make a breakthrough. It would be great to be known around the world. The Japanese mass media ignores us and tries not to make us be known. We want the world to know us.

SHIO OKAWA

By now it's obvious that all we'll get in Japan is the silent treatment.

JOHN LENNON

It comes down to missionary work, to be renown around the world.

SHIO OKAWA

We need to make a breakthrough somewhere outside of Japan.

JOHN LENNON

That's right. Let's make it happen wherever it will happen from. Let's do our best. Yes.

SHIO OKAWA

Thank you very much.

2

The Thought that John Lennon Put into His Music

China needs to let music and the arts spread in their country

SHIO OKAWA

We would like to ask him (John Lennon) questions regarding China.

RYUHO OKAWA

Alright then. Mr. John Lennon, could we ask you additional questions? Mr. John Lennon, could we ask you additional questions? Mr. John Lennon, could we ask you additional questions?

[*Approximately five seconds of silence pass.*]

JOHN LENNON

Yes.

SHIO OKAWA

At the time, you were banned from selling your Beatles albums in Asian countries ruled by one-party dictatorships, such as the People's Republic of China and the Republic of Korea. How do you feel about this?

JOHN LENNON

The same problem still exists today, doesn't it? They won't let American culture or Japanese culture in, will they? They disguise themselves as democracies, but their systems are totalitarian and are run by the rule of persons, aren't they?

SHIO OKAWA

Right.

JOHN LENNON

How can they accept our political principles or election systems if they won't even let in our music and movies? This needs to be torn down. Don't make the mistake of thinking they are on the side of justice. Japan's left-wing groups insist that China, North Korea, and South Korea are right so Japan is the one that needs to repent, but in the end, countries that won't let in Japanese, American, or even British cultures are not in their right minds.

Look at Hong Kong. It's a Chinese-speaking territory so you would expect they would be glad to be returned to the mainland after 150 years of colonial rule under England. But instead of being happy about it, they don't like it. They started the Umbrella Revolution. Of course, Master Okawa's lecture tour* there

---

* On May 22, 2011, in Hong Kong, Ryuho Okawa held a lecture in English entitled, "The Fact and the Truth," and said to the Hong Kong people that they must become the leaders of China. He asked them to teach and lead the people of China and show them the direction that China should move toward. See Ryuho Okawa, *Love for the Future* (New York: IRH Press, 2019).

influenced that, but we also worked to make it happen.

There are countries where Christianity is facing banning or suppression that are on the verge of coming under complete regulation. Chinese President Xi Jinping will hold the power to appoint the bishops of the Catholic Church in China.* The Vatican won't be able to oppose him from doing so if it could lead to Christian persecution.

China is working to take Hong Kong and Taiwan in the same way. We are fighting against this. You're also fighting this as a religion, but so is Christianity. Their countries also need to be changed so that music and the arts can come in. How can there be so many mobile phones and smartphones and yet there is no freedom? That's why we have to "rock" the place somehow.

---

* On September 22, 2018, the Vatican announced that they reached a provisional agreement regarding the issue of appointing bishops in China. It included the Vatican's acknowledgment of the seven bishops of the Chinese Patriotic Catholic Association.

SHIO OKAWA

Yes, you're right.

Governmental control of cultural expression is secretly keeping Chinese people under control

SHIO OKAWA

I've heard that when you made the album *Imagine*, you never expressed public support for any political party. Instead, you said that power should reside with the people. And you organized a march.

JOHN LENNON

"Power to the People?"

SHIO OKAWA

Right. Your album is speculated to be about prison violence, race, gender-equality, Northern Ireland conflicts, and other things. On the cover of your album, *Sometime in New York City*, you placed a montage of Mao Zedong and Richard Nixon dancing naked together.

JOHN LENNON

What we have is countries ruled by atheism in the name of totalitarianism, or rule by persons. They're being run by a fake "living god." The people don't realize they're living under the governmental control of cultural expression.

SHIO OKAWA

I see. That's true.

JOHN LENNON

We need to tear this down. It was a wall even the Beatles could not tear down. If it had been Tolstoy, he would have done it through a revival of Christianity. The Russian Orthodox Church is finally experiencing a revival now. For seventy years, the country (as the former Soviet Union) was communist, and the opposite of what Tolstoy envisioned. It took a while didn't it.

So it is going to take time and you probably can't foresee what will happen one hundred years later in the twenty-second century, but you are planting the seeds right now.

SHIO OKAWA
Yes. You're right.

JOHN LENNON
Yeah. Something else will come into being in the twenty-second century. You are sowing the seeds for that right now. You need to plant seeds in all kinds of fields.

Even when countries recognize the truth, they are looking the other way

JOHN LENNON

You should call for more freedom in music, in the arts, and film, too. China is constantly bashing Japan and creating movies that depict Japan as being evil to say that defeating Japan is justice. You're not permitted to praise Japan and it's the same way in South Korea as well as in North Korea. It's not possible to have a dialogue with them. There is a need to let them know that it is their country that is not right.

Uyghur, Mongolia, and Tibet are teaching us about that, but the world pretends not to see. Muslims around the world should unite and say something about the plight of their own people in Uyghur but they stay silent out of fear of China. They are more afraid of losing trade and money from China.

This is the state of the world. That is why there has to be a revolution in China. It's the same in Thailand, isn't it?

My support swings toward the right wing or the left wing as necessary

SHIO OKAWA

Lastly, you began to call more loudly for peace and the end of wars because of the Vietnam War. Could you explain what that was about?

JOHN LENNON

There were a lot of complex issues involved. From America's perspective, it appeared as if communism would spread to the world in a domino effect, so they had to stop it in Vietnam. The result was China-backed North Vietnam's victory. It was partially because Americans were not very good at guerilla warfare.

Some things need to be decided by yourselves, you know. Communism was supposed to take over all of Vietnam, but instead, it changed. Now Vietnam is strengthening ties with the free world, right? Give people freedom, and they will pursue what they ought to pursue. Vietnam is now at odds with China and seeking Japan's help. War is not the only means for settling conflicts.

Fighting against communism was a good cause. But if being against communism was a good enough cause by itself, the Tripartite Pact between Japan, Germany, and Italy was also a bulwark against communism. But they were defeated, weren't they? So war does not determine everything.

In that situation, Vietnam's autonomy should have been respected. Also, you could not expect the world's democrats to tolerate the burning of farmers and other innocent citizens with Napalm. The Vietnam War, the anti-war movement, the civil rights movement, and women's liberation all occurred at the time America's arrogance from its victory in World War II reached its peak. These were problems that were jolting the times. So we can swing whether to the left wing or to the right wing, depending on what's being needed.

We have many means on hand to tear down China's regime

JOHN LENNON

Protecting freedom and capitalism is okay but, how should I put this, watching farmers in braided bamboo hats being killed with modern weapons was unbearable for everyone. The age of television had already started, you know. It was unbearable to watch. It was so sad. How could you do this and then continue to regard Japan as guilty?

Japan's army was much stronger. It took control over Asia easily. America was much less efficient. They conducted a massacre in a sloppy way. They killed millions of people and still couldn't gain control. The reason is because they held their lives too dear. They relied on weapons so they wouldn't have to put their lives in danger. They still have that tendency.

Even now America is developing aside from nuclear weapons MOABs (Massive Ordnance Air Blasts), a weapon of mass destruction. It can suck out all of the oxygen in a five hundred-meter radius, killing all life in its range. China succeeded in testing this weapon recently, didn't they?

SHIO OKAWA
Yes.

JOHN LENNON
It's obvious that they mean it as a threat to Taiwan. They're saying, "Taiwan would disappear in an instant if we dropped this on you." "We can drop

this on Hong Kong too, and also on Japan." "It doesn't need to be a nuclear weapon."

Drop it on to a metropolitan city. A five hundred-meter radius would mean the deaths of a hundred thousand people. The impact would be immense. Imagine if it was dropped above the Prime Minister's office. Times like that are coming again. That's why we are in a hurry.

We are using every means to demolish that rigid, stiff system to make it a more fluid one in which different opinions can be expressed and things can be done differently. If we need to use music for that, we'll use it, and if we need UFOs, then we'll use that, too. Space beings will appear if need be, too. Space beings have appeared above an airport in China before. So, there you have it. That's our thinking.

SHIO OKAWA
I understand.

JOHN LENNON

Hahaha [*laughs*].

I wanted to extend a helping hand to Japan, the victim of atomic bombings

JOHN LENNON

Is there anything else you forgot to ask?

SHIO OKAWA

There is one more thing. It may have been because you were married to Yoko Ono, but you visited Japan quite frequently.

JOHN LENNON

Yes, that's right.

SHIO OKAWA

As someone connected to Jesus Christ, your visit to Japan…

JOHN LENNON

Yes. I also had a lot of fans in Japan. Japan is a country on which the atomic bomb was dropped twice, in Hiroshima and Nagasaki. It may have happened in ancient times, but at least in these two thousand years of history that everyone is familiar with, it's the only country that has had that happen to it. I wanted to extend a hand of salvation to this country.

SHIO OKAWA

Thank you very much.

JOHN LENNON

Yeah, yes. In order that it won't happen again. Militarism is okay if it is for national defense, but when it turns into imperialism and other countries are invaded, then you've gone too far. But every country has the possibility of doing that.

I came here to console Japan. There can be a Jesus Christ like me, too. There could be a "weird" Buddha too, you know?

WADA

[*Laughs.*]

Citizens living under communism wanted to get a taste of Western culture

SHIO OKAWA

But I see now that the reason why the Beatles' songs were banned from communist countries like the Soviet Union, East Germany, or dictatorships like China and the Republic of Korea was because Jesus Christ was trying to get these countries to go in the opposite direction they were going in through music.

JOHN LENNON

Yes! It might have had something to do with the communist regime collapsing in Eastern Europe, and the East joining the West. They felt there was something wrong with a country that doesn't allow you to have what you want, right?

Unable to escape nor import what they want, they felt there must be something wrong with their country. So, creating something they will want is one way…

SHIO OKAWA
Ohhh! I see.

JOHN LENNON
To make them feel, "I want that," "I want to listen to that," "I want to feel what it's like living in the West." I might have looked like I was siding with the communists in my activism against the Vietnam War, but it wasn't because I approved of communism. We act as needed, you know.

We'll point out it's wrong when someone goes too far. There are a lot of problems today too, all kinds, including environmental problems, so it's difficult, but oh well. You just have to deal with them as they come.

When shown footage of the atomic bombings, Putin made the sign of the cross whereas Obama clapped in applause

JOHN LENNON

You're going up against Mao Zedong and Xi Jinping right? Well you have to don't you, otherwise a great dictator, a dictator with control over 1.4 billion people will take over other countries too. That is a terrible thing. A frightful thing.

SHIO OKAWA

The world needs to wake up to this danger, doesn't it?

JOHN LENNON

To use 1.4 billion people to be in control of over at least three billion of the world's population is terrifying. So yes, you do have to voice criticism about that. You're trying to be friendly with Russia, right? I think greater liberalization and democratization need to be advanced within that country.

SHIO OKAWA

President Putin is trying to revive the Russian Orthodox Church. Also, when he saw footage of the atomic bombing*...

JOHN LENNON

Yes, that's right. He cried, didn't he?

SHIO OKAWA

...he made a sign of the cross.

---

* On June 6, 2014, in France, during the ceremony of the seventieth anniversary of D-Day, footages of the atomic bombings on Japan were shown. The news broadcasted Russian President Vladimir Putin who was in attendance making the sign of the cross as he watched.

JOHN LENNON

That's a good thing. That's another thing you need to make clear.

SHIO OKAWA

Yes. On the other hand, while you would expect Barack Obama to be a pacifist against the use of atomic bombs, footage showed him clapping in applause.

JOHN LENNON

He applauded? Well, reactions vary, it seems.

President Trump is also a rock 'n' roller

JOHN LENNON

What we are seeing now is that the victorious nations from the last war that became permanent members of the United Nations are now about to enter a war over supremacy. The winners who became the permanent members of the

Security Council were from both the Free World and the communist bloc. The Soviet Union and China were in there, and the others were the United States, Britain, and France right? But Britain is about to leave the EU and France is weakened.

And the United States is a divided nation, with some people believing they are being run by an insane President. There are Angels of Light amongst those that think that way and also among those who support Mr. Trump. It's hard to understand what he's doing. He is probably such a big president whose evaluation will be left to later generations. I imagine it's hard to make a clear judgment about him. When he said he would build a wall on the border with Mexico, the Vatican spoke out against him saying that, but the Vatican isn't going to stop drugs from coming into America, are they?

SHIO OKAWA

I guess you could say Mr. Trump is also a rocker [*laughs*].

JOHN LENNON

He is a rocker. The Pope went to Mexico. It would have been nice if he had said, "Stop the illegal immigration. Stop smuggling drugs. Then I'll convince Mr. Trump." But instead, he said the Christian calling is "not to raise walls but bridges." But with a bridge, only more will come in.

SHIO OKAWA

He failed to address the root problem, the reason why Mr. Trump is building a wall.

JOHN LENNON

You have to admit there is a very religious motive behind it. Drug-related corruption and illegal immigration are creating a hotbed for crime. He doesn't want to see America turning into Gotham City*, right? He has a religious motive. But people do not understand that. So that's the hard part.

"All we can do is sing, but we will support you"

JOHN LENNON

If we rock 'n' rollers were out there, alive today, we might dislike someone like Mr. Trump. We might regard him as a rabid dog. The world is watching how crazy he'll be. A man who can go head to head with CNN is quite interesting, you know. His "craziness" is also what is making North Korea fear him. China, too. It makes them worry what he'll do if he gets really mad.

---

* Gotham City is a fictional, crime-filled city appearing in the American comic book series, Batman.

SHIO OKAWA

Yes, you don't know what he'll do.

JOHN LENNON

Right, there's that. It's because of his craziness. China cannot win if they make him mad and go to war with the United States. They are stalling for time, working on taking control of countries in Asia without upsetting the United States. So, you are fighting against this. You should do a good job. All we can do is sing, but we will support you, too.

SHIO OKAWA

Yes. We look forward to that. Thank you.

CHAPTER TWO

The Power of Music

John Lennon's Spiritual Message Part 2

Originally recorded in Japanese on January 21, 2019,
in the Special Lecture Hall of Happy Science in Japan,
and later translated into English.

Interviewers from Happy Science

Shio Okawa
Aide to Master & CEO

Sakurako Jinmu
Managing Director
Chief Secretary of the First Secretarial Division
    Religious Affairs Headquarters

The opinions of the spirit do not necessarily reflect those of Happy Science Group.
For the mechanism behind spiritual messages, see the end section.

Interviewers are listed in the order that they appear in the transcript.
 Their professional titles represent their positions at the time of the interview.

1

The Power of Music that Can Destroy Social Structures

John Lennon's receivers are fleeing

SHIO OKAWA
Who is this?

JOHN LENNON
Yeah.

JINMU
Who is this?

JOHN LENNON
We are right now applying pressure.

SHIO OKAWA
Are you "the Beatles"?

JOHN LENNON

Yup. We are trying to create our receivers, but they are fleeing.

SHIO OKAWA

So, some of our current staff's *ikiryo** spirits are intruding?

JOHN LENNON

They don't like it because it's heavy. They hate it because it's too heavy. They are fine with something a bit smaller.

SHIO OKAWA

Are you John Lennon? McCartney?

JOHN LENNON

Yeah. It's John Lennon. Even if I try to make a song, they hate it because if they receive it, they may possibly break down. They don't want

---

* An *ikiryo* is the combination of a person's strong thoughts and his or her guardian spirit.

to hear it. Usually, everyone around the world would want to listen to my songs, but your disciples (the staff members of Happy Science) do not want to hear them because they would have to work very hard.

SHIO OKAWA

But it's their task to find someone who can sing those songs.

JINMU

By thinking that they have to sell a hundred million copies?

SHIO OKAWA

If not in English… well, someone sings an English song in *Panda Roonda*.

JOHN LENNON

No, they want me to sell myself at another music company, not Happy Science. That's it. That's what they are thinking.

SHIO OKAWA
Why? Why?

JOHN LENNON
Because they don't have enough ability and experience. They have a long way to go.

SHIO OKAWA
We know that.

JOHN LENNON
They are really targeting somewhere around 1,000 to 10,000 copies. When it comes to what they make, they can only sell 1,000 copies at most. So, a hundred million seem far-fetched to them. To them, I seem like a troublemaker that they don't want to see.

SHIO OKAWA
I don't understand.

JOHN LENNON

Well, it's true. The disciples are like that.

SHIO OKAWA

That's why they don't sell.

There's a huge difference in the scale of thinking between Master Okawa and his disciples

JOHN LENNON

The disciples can't bear the load unless it's reduced to one-hundredth of Master's thinking. There's just too much of a difference between Master Okawa and them. That's the problem. The same goes for the report from International Headquarters. They can't do something unless it's one-hundredth the scale Master Okawa does. If he does an event for fifty thousand people, then the disciples will do it for five hundred people. If he does it for ten thousand, then they will do it for a hundred.

SHIO OKAWA

But... How many years later will the movie be released?

JINMU

I don't think it's been decided yet.

SHIO OKAWA

Probably about six years from now, right?

JOHN LENNON

Yeah. They're saying I don't need to send any more (spiritual messages).

SHIO OKAWA

But it isn't anything to worry about so much.

JOHN LENNON

No, no, that's not what I mean. The person in charge wants my spiritual message to be stored away and the music based on it to be made somewhere he cannot see. That's what this is about.

SHIO OKAWA

Why does he hate it? Happy Science will go under and everyone will be on the streets without a source of income.

JOHN LENNON

The disciples have absolutely no brains to think about the following year.

SHIO OKAWA

Why?

JOHN LENNON

You ask why, but that's what ordinary people are like.

SHIO OKAWA

Well, I guess if you get to that position, that's how you become.

JOHN LENNON

So, if you become a manager for John Lennon or the Beatles, you will go crazy. John Lennon isn't welcome, as far as the disciples are concerned. All they need are guardian spirits of lower-level singers than me, in Japan. So, we are being resisted.

JINMU

But we've been receiving spiritual messages from you and others all this time, so why?

JOHN LENNON

That's because he wasn't at his current position.

SHIO OKAWA

Huh? The audience would appreciate it if they could listen to good songs. Really...

JOHN LENNON

Well, the audience would, as you say. The audience is like that.

SHIO OKAWA

It would rather be unpleasant if we were made to listen to a song that the disciples made themselves and that even our believers would think will not be a hit among the general public. At the very least, we would like to listen to a pure song.

JOHN LENNON

The audience would, yes. But the group of staff members would not. The group of staff members wants to make sure they can be paid.

SHIO OKAWA

If the disciples did work that was suited to their work ability, they would not be paid their wages. That's why Master Okawa is really trying hard to create high-level contents. When these go through the disciples, the content level ultimately drops, but since it is high to begin with, everyone can be paid their wages.

JOHN LENNON

Yeah. So, the disciples rented a hotel in Thailand and gathered people, screened the movie *The Laws of the Universe-Part I*, showed a DVD of Master's English lecture "What is 'Truth'?," served a meal, and had them go home. That's the type of work the disciples are doing; they are working on a slightly small scale. Even though there are so many of them. The scale of thinking is so vastly different. In reality, they only preach about five minutes. That's what they are doing. That's the reality. So, disciples would be troubled if their work were large. Master is trying to make a breakthrough somehow because he wants to spread the Truth to the whole planet, but the disciples are only thinking about how they can live through today, live through this year, and live through next year. The higher the level demanded, the more they disappear off to somewhere.

"Our job was to appeal to the general public"

SHIO OKAWA
The artist Sae Shinohara sings a song in a Happy Science movie that came from Jesus.*

JOHN LENNON
Yeah. But it's not a hit.

SHIO OKAWA
It's not a hit, but it will definitely be handed down to later generations.

---

* This is referring to the song titled, "Heart to Heart," from the documentary movie called, *Heart to Heart.*

JOHN LENNON

Well, about one thousand copies at the most. Even if Jesus sang it, the CD will only sell one thousand copies.

SHIO OKAWA

But really, disciples should not reject it even before someone sings it.

JINMU

We haven't even received it yet.

JOHN LENNON

That's why I'm saying it's heavy. It's okay if Jesus is the one sending it, because he isn't a singer.

SHIO OKAWA

Oh! I see. If they are told that a song is from John Lennon, they need to be more serious in...

JOHN LENNON

That's why it's a problem for them. Because they would think they have to sell a hundred million, or at least ten million. Otherwise, they think people would feel it's fake, which distresses them. They are fine with a song from John Lennon's cousin, for example. So, we are being resisted.

SHIO OKAWA

But if it's a theme song by John Lennon, then even if the movie is watched only by our believers, that would still be okay because the Happy Science brand would be enhanced more. If we use something of a lower level...

JOHN LENNON

Staff members are perfectly fine with songs that can be written and composed by the staff. So, the general public cannot understand how good the songs are. The disciples are just making arrangements about who inside their group to invite and ask for offerings from. That's what they have been doing all this time. But we, the Beatles, didn't have an organized group of followers, so our work was to appeal to the general public. The opposite phenomenon could be occurring with the disciples, where they are reducing their work in order to stabilize their salary. Namie Amuro didn't have such a group either, so she was able to retire. Good for her. She was able to quit.

SHIO OKAWA

Hmm.

JOHN LENNON

If she had needed to run an organized group or a company, then it would've been tough for her. It's a bit like that, you know? Just imagine Namie Amuro having a company and employing a thousand staff members to conduct a tour. That's what Happy Science currently is like. Yeah.

The organization of disciples at Happy Science is like an agency that only collects commission

SHIO OKAWA

I mean, I understand. But if so, then they should just give up and make music faithfully in accordance with the original songs made by Master Okawa. Something he considers good.

JOHN LENNON

No, that's not it. You have to read the meaning behind their "no." It means, "If you want it so much, then sing it yourself." That's what they are saying.

SHIO OKAWA

Wow, that's horrible.

JOHN LENNON

That's how disciples are. That's them. That's the way for them to live.

SHIO OKAWA

"If you want it so much, then sing it yourself"...

JOHN LENNON

"Sing it yourself. If you can't sing it, then don't make it." That's what they're saying. [*About five seconds of silence pass.*] So, the Beatles or John Lennon is too big a name.

SHIO OKAWA

No, I mean, Master's...

JOHN LENNON

But when I came as a religious figure, I was able to (create songs).

SHIO OKAWA

It would be fine to have someone who's not a believer sing, as long as he or she could sing.

JOHN LENNON

The disciples didn't know the truth about the religious figure, so it was okay.

SHIO OKAWA

I mean, Lord Alpha's theme* and "Lost Love"† are sung by the same person who is not our believer.

JOHN LENNON

Hmm.

SHIO OKAWA

But if you listen, you can tell that he sings knowing what the contents are. We have to leave a legacy of Master Okawa's creations somehow, even if this is the only way. I understand well

---

* This is referring to an insert song from the movie, *The Laws of the Universe-Part I*, entitled, "The Beginning (Alpha's Theme)."

† This is referring to an insert song from the movie, *The Laws of the Universe-Part 0*.

that the disciples are only at that level, but if so, they should give up and think of a way to leave a legacy of what Master Okawa considers good, otherwise it will all be meaningless.

JOHN LENNON

In short, disciples are an agency. It's an organization where they collect commission just by distributing work. [*About ten seconds of silence pass.*] Well… Well, it's such a pity. The only job disciples have is to be a stone wall. With a stone wall, you might simply catch eels that live in holes between the stones. Well, unfortunately it seems I'm not so welcomed. Even someone like Ryunosuke Akutagawa is not welcomed, either. His level is too high. It seems like they want something that's more in line with the trend.

SHIO OKAWA

But we mustn't forget the audience's point of view.

JOHN LENNON

Hmm. Well, Master is working hard by himself, but everyone else is unable to receive that. So, although they are talking about the Academy Award, they're all thinking that it's better not to win it.

SHIO OKAWA

Ah, they probably are.

JOHN LENNON

Deep down. They think, "Things will get complicated and we will be busy. The level required of us will get higher as time goes on, so no thank you." They're aiming for the same level of work as they did the year before. That's what they're thinking. Master alone is thinking he wants to be known throughout the world, but the disciples are thinking that they cannot make that happen with their abilities. That's what happens when they see less and less people come to their events. Master sees many people come to his event, so he thinks it will be like that, but the disciples already see and know that only a few would come if they were to hold an event. They know very well. You cannot turn them into one hundred Namie Amuro's.

SHIO OKAWA
I wouldn't ask them to become Namie Amuro's, of course. There might be one charismatic person in every ten thousand or so.

JOHN LENNON
Hmm. Honestly, they're better at being hated than being liked.

"There's no need for the disciples.
Master Okawa should do what he wants to do."

SHIO OKAWA

There will be no meaning for the disciples existing unless they at least try to receive and create what Master wants to create, with as transparent a heart as possible, even if they're not full of charisma.

JOHN LENNON

So, he doesn't need them (the disciples), I think. In fact, it would be better if he does what he wants to do.

SHIO OKAWA

Maybe so.

JOHN LENNON

There's no need for them. The problem is that everything has to go through them. As I look at Happy Science, what you need to do is to withdraw. He is developing the group in many different genres, but they're all led by people who can't make them grow. So, the simplest way is for Master to just do what he can by himself. He doesn't need the others, basically.

SHIO OKAWA

At this point, it's a matter of leaving behind what Master did in his lifetime, as much as possible.

JOHN LENNON

Though he writes the stories and original scripts for movies, it's very hard for the disciples to write screenplays based on those. They would have a breakdown, right?

This means he needs a screenwriter who can support himself or produce a hit. Really, it takes that much to make Happy Science even bigger. If you can get such a person, you'll be able to develop Master's original story into something that a lot more people would want to see. That's what the disciples are being asked of. However, the fact is that he is letting them practice how to write. You can see similar cases all over. The local temples are probably in a similar situation. He can have his lectures recorded and shown at local temples, but since the temple managers don't have the ability to comment on them, believers just watch them and go home. It's sad. How shall I express it? We know a bit about how songs or other things really can fanatically and instantly spread throughout the world, and how Master's lectures can also spread fanatically. But the disciples became a hindrance to the progress of Happy Science. This goes for Christianity and other groups as well. It's the disciples who stumble. They stumble, really.

We were the first to hold a concert at a baseball stadium. Master gave lectures at a baseball stadium, but he has nowhere beyond that to aim for in terms of his own work. Nothing beyond that. The next stage is whether the organization can spread this movement. That's where he is struggling. If he gets involved in organizational management, it will prevent him from focusing on production activities and receiving inspiration frequently.

Disciples want to work at a level they are comfortable with

JOHN LENNON
So, you know... they think that if they are going to sing a song given by the Beatles, then they should just let the ghost do the singing and air that. They're not musicians, so I guess they can't play the guitar and sing as we did. It can't be helped.

SHIO OKAWA
But the movie will be screened six or seven

years later, so the insert song may be sung by someone we don't know yet. He or she in sixth or seventh grade right now may be singing it in the future.

JOHN LENNON

Japan is a small country, so people tend to grow smaller and refuse to go outside. They can't make it out of Japan. Everything is like that nowadays.

SHIO OKAWA

We are now being allowed to live in the same age as Master. Even if we aren't able to leave his legacy in tangible form, if we could pass down his philosophy, artistic view, concept behind his works, and things like that, then later on, someone better at it will create it, I hope.

JOHN LENNON

You might have positive thinking like that, but some people, like Master's son, think that if Master didn't work, they could do his work instead.

SHIO OKAWA
Hmm, yeah, you're right.

JOHN LENNON
Uh huh. (They think in) the same way.

SHIO OKAWA
So, the issue our Media Division is also facing...

JOHN LENNON
They want to work at a level they are capable of working, and their doing so will destroy the company.

SHIO OKAWA
If they're going to send out thoughts like that while they're living in the same age as Master, then they should just keep silent.

JOHN LENNON

If they were to run companies by themselves, they would fail because they bring no added value. They reduce Master's work to one-hundredth its value, so they get by without having to go in the red. It's a business that will eventually come to an end. Well... I guess they didn't need a song from the Beatles. Hmm. It's too bad, really. We feel that Ryuho Okawa deserves to receive our inspiration, but Happy Science doesn't have such caliber. It's too bad.

"The level of Bodhisattva is not as easy as you think"

JINMU

If you were to send us a song through inspiration, what would you require of the singer?

JOHN LENNON

I'll need someone who is at least about Namie Amuro's level as an artist. Someone younger would be fine, too. Male or female, the singer should be someone of her level. Otherwise, they can't be Master's right hand. If they could at least spread Happy Science through songs or shows, then that's fine, but if they're just going to use the songs to make their own debut or to force your believers into buying, then they're just amateurs working for their own pleasure. It's comparable to an IT company in Shibuya, with about four employees. Many people run companies and go bankrupt in three years, but such people have no skill, so it can't be helped. There are only such people (at Happy Science). People with skills are doing other work. It's sad, but the same thing happened in Jesus' time; his disciples were not so competent. And from his viewpoint, the current church system is not so desirable. He thinks that the churches are doing the exact opposite, and that what they are doing is totally different from his teachings. They work as a "tax office." Also, they're working like politicians, which is strange. Jesus would probably go as far as to light them on fire, an act similar to his driving out the Pharisees. He would probably say it's not what they should be doing. This is the level of disciples, unfortunately.

The level of a bodhisattva is not that easy to attain. It's not easy at all. Everyone thinks they are at the bodhisattva level, but it's not that easy to reach. At the bodhisattva's level, a religion can only be established in the generations (after the founder), so it's not as easy as they think. They're not at that level yet. They are at a far lower level. Much, much lower. Many disciples are thinking they are bodhisattvas or tathagatas, but they're at a level where they have just gotten past the fifth dimension*, you know? They're somewhere near the base of Takamagahara.

The majority of disciples are thinking that, "If Master is thinking about having the next leader take over his work, maybe we should not expand our group too much, otherwise we might go bankrupt." They don't want Master to do anything rapid and huge. He doesn't go to the local temples to see how things are going. He would probably let out a big sigh. They work efficiently, you know? It's really amazing because they finish a day's job in just ten or twenty minutes. They don't work all day long.

SHIO OKAWA

When he gives a lecture at a local temple, although it may be a small one, leader members from adjacent temples could also fit in that temple.

---

* In the other world, also called the spirit world, the place where each soul resides depends on the soul's degree of faith and enlightenment. On planet Earth, the spirit world stretches from the fourth-dimensional Astral Realm to the ninth-dimensional Cosmic Realm. Souls possessing benevolent hearts live in the fifth-dimensional world, bodhisattvas and angels of altruistic hearts live in the seventh-dimensional world, and messiahs, such as Shakyamuni Buddha and Jesus Christ, live in the ninth-dimensional world.

JOHN LENNON

They have such easy jobs. Bringing new people applies to us singers, too. We booked many baseball stadiums for our concerts, and in order to have them there, we needed to get new people, new fans. But Master's disciples don't sufficiently understand what it means to use contents created by him to get such people. So, I'm saying that having created an organization is working to his disadvantage. They may say they're spreading the teachings, but they're doing something totally different. I think the truth is that they're conducting ritual prayers and such to bring in enough money for them to get paid. Well, I think there's already a huge gap between Master and disciples. I guess they're like a wholesale store, but they're saying they can't be a wholesale store for the Beatles.

The disciples will first say "no." They start with that. This is a bureaucratic nature. Rock bands like us destroy such things, that's our basic idea. We need to totally destroy such things.

SHIO OKAWA

That's true. The Beatles was something like a revolution.

JOHN LENNON

Yup. It's total destruction. It's the Storming of the Bastille.*

The significance of
John Lennon's assassination

SHIO OKAWA

By the way, I'd like to ask you something else since we're lucky enough to have you here today.

---

* On July 14, 1789, French citizens seized the military fortress and prison of Bastille. This came to be called the Storming of the Bastille and was when the French Revolution started.

It'll add more value to the session. I hear often that when John Lennon was assassinated, there must have been the Grim Reaper, but was that true? You said you are a branch spirit of Jesus, so I can't imagine the Grim Reaper coming for you. Was your death already decided on in the heavenly world?

JOHN LENNON

I was basically raising my children for about five years. I did housework and childrearing for about five years, and was assassinated the month after my new album was released. I was assassinated, so I guess I was told to "rest in peace" [*laughs*]. I finished my work in about two or three years. We started around 1962, the peak came quickly in about three or four years, and we were done by 1969 or so. I lived until 1980, but I was killing time. People said that I displayed a lot of odd behavior and that I was becoming strange.

SHIO OKAWA

I think you changed a bit when you went to India.

JOHN LENNON

Yeah, I did.

SHIO OKAWA

What did you gain in India?

JOHN LENNON

In India, I learned what it is to be a hippie. Be a hippie.

SHIO OKAWA

I see.

JOHN LENNON

I studied up on that. I was fed up with a British gentleman's way of thinking, their "set" way of thinking, and being chased by the police.

Whenever we had a concert, our fans would run around, so the police had to chase them down. I just hated performing and singing while seeing this. I thought, "Why does it happen every time?" And when the concert ended, an armored car came inside the baseball stadium to pick us up and flee from the fans. This happened over and over again, and in the end, we were done. We were done and there wasn't any medium larger than that at that time, so we couldn't do anything more. We didn't have an organization, either. We weren't able to do anything about these people, the avid fans. Maybe some bands can deal with such kind of fans better now, but there is a limit to what they can do, too.

SHIO OKAWA

The Beatles was the first rock band to hold a concert at a baseball stadium.

JOHN LENNON

Yes, that's right.

SHIO OKAWA

The Beatles was also the first rock band to hold a concert at Nippon Budokan.

JOHN LENNON

And Master Okawa held a lecture event there. Amazing! He can do it at the Tokyo Dome, right? A lecture there.

SHIO OKAWA

As his disciples, it makes us deeply emotional just thinking about the fact that Master is working right after Jesus.

JOHN LENNON

Well, I'm not Jesus himself. John Lennon was assassinated in December 1980. Master Ryuho

Okawa attained enlightenment in March 1981. There were only three months between the two. You know? The baton was successfully passed down.

SHIO OKAWA

I see.

JOHN LENNON

So there was a reason behind the assassination as well.

SHIO OKAWA

In our spiritual interviews with Yaidron,* he said that the Grim Reaper could have been near the person who was assassinated, and that even if this wasn't the case, there may have been people in the heavenly world who planned it.

---

* Yaidron is a space being who was discovered through a UFO reading conducted by the author. He comes from Planet Elder, a sister planet of Planet Zeta, and is from the reptilian race. Physically, he has white-colored skin similar to the Caucasians on Earth, is handsome-looking, and is also double-horned. He is giving his protection to El Cantare, who has incarnated to this physical world and is currently living. See "UFO Reading" held on August 19, 2018.

JOHN LENNON

I'm the only member of the Beatles who was assassinated. I was targeted [*laughs*]. But I guess some people didn't want to see John Lennon at sixty or seventy.

The power in the songs by the Beatles

JOHN LENNON

I left McCartney to be my missionary. A missionary...

SHIO OKAWA

So, Paul McCartney has a mission even now?

JOHN LENNON

Yeah. I left him to be my missionary. My work was already done. Well, it may have seemed to overlap with the anti-Vietnam War movement. Songs by the Beatles have the power to destroy movements like the past wars that the U.S. was involved in such as the Gulf War and the Iraq War, as well as the Soviet-Afghan War, and even the wars to come.

But we didn't acknowledge imperialism either, which you are all against. That's why our songs never made it into China, North Korea, or South Korea. Countries without freedom, democracy, and faith block our songs. Our works don't spread into those countries. Perhaps we became even more hippie-like after we went to India.

In advanced countries, initially, everything was good; the fans were screaming for us. But we went from a social phenomenon to a social turmoil, and a lot of people were arrested or got into accidents. After marrying Yoko Ono, I was criticized too. Some Caucasians said that I changed a bit. It was also during the racial liberation movement, which was the trend back then.

SHIO OKAWA

So, that means you, a branch spirit of Jesus, were living in the same age as Martin Luther King, Jr.

JOHN LENNON

Yeah, yeah. Same time. The same age as the Black Emancipation Movement.

SHIO OKAWA

In those days in the U.S., it was natural to have racially segregated concerts, but you said, "Abolish racial segregation at concerts, otherwise we won't perform."

JOHN LENNON

Oh, yeah I did.

SHIO OKAWA

You seemed like a pacifist with your "Love and Peace," almost as if you were a leftist, but considering you couldn't sell your records in China and other imperialist or communist countries...

JOHN LENNON

Yeah, that's right. Yeah. I couldn't sell them to the former Soviet Union and its communist, satellite states.

SHIO OKAWA

Seeing that, you weren't just a leftist engaging in peace activities.

JOHN LENNON

We brought trouble; we were like a signal that marked the destruction of regimes, so any government run by a single entity where the people are under control or total suppression didn't like us. So, we had power in us.

SHIO OKAWA

I felt as though you denied systems where people were bound or deprived of freedom, and denied wars that tried to take over another country.

JOHN LENNON

I mean, even in Uyghur today, if everyone were to get together and sing "Let It Be" as they pleased, "it" will crumble.

SHIO OKAWA

"It" meaning China's strategy?

JOHN LENNON

Yeah, yeah. It will crumble.

"I was assassinated by a white person, not the Grim Reaper"

JOHN LENNON

Politics and music aren't so different from each other. They're closer than you may think. The same goes for movies. There are many movies that aren't shown. Any movie that portrays Japan positively isn't shown in South Korea or China. Same thing with music. History is rewritten. This is a difficult matter, very difficult. You must be suffering right now. It must be difficult.

For example, next week, or is it this week? Master will give a lecture in Hiroshima[*], right? Now, who should be the one to blame, those who dropped the atomic bomb or those who got the atomic bomb dropped on? Neither side will ever come to an agreement. I mean, I eventually married Yoko Ono, but she's Japanese. Americans

---

[*] Ryuho Okawa held a lecture entitled, "Hope for the Future," on January 26, 2019, at the Hiroshima Prefectural Culture and Arts Hall.

feel that the Japanese have original sin, so they cannot accept a musical hero marrying a Japanese. They think, "The Japanese are human beings that deserve to be massacred. They must be that kind of a race."

SHIO OKAWA

You mean that the Americans needed a reason for dropping the atomic bombs?

JOHN LENNON

Yeah, yeah, yeah. The Japanese are a race where one hundred thousand or perhaps three hundred thousand people must be killed. That's how it has to be. They are thinking, "John Lennon, who is active in the antiwar movement is marrying a Japanese, which means he will start saying that it was wrong to drop the atomic bomb on Japan during WWII." So, they want to kill. I was assassinated by a white person, not the Grim Reaper.

JINMU

You mean, a Caucasian?

SHIO OKAWA

A Caucasian who racially discriminated…

JOHN LENNON

He believed in white supremacy. The most active ones are the KKK.* They are the most active.

SHIO OKAWA

You were against it and…

JOHN LENNON

I was against it.

SHIO OKAWA

As a result, you were assassinated.

---

* The Ku Klux Klan, also called the KKK, is an American secret society of white supremacists formed after the Civil War, which violently discriminates against African Americans, Asians, and people of other races.

JOHN LENNON

I married Yoko Ono, was influenced by India, and became a bit of a lunatic, so they wanted to kill me even more.

"The three demons" in the eyes of John Lennon

SHIO OKAWA

You said you were a branch spirit of Jesus. Considering that and the fact that you were with Yoko Ono, I sense a kind of connection. Japan fought against Western Allies, which had established faith in Jesus, but a branch spirit of Jesus married a Japanese. There must be some meaning in this.

JOHN LENNON

Yeah, that's right. Americans want to keep believing that crushing Japan in WWII was a good thing. And on top of that, regarding the Vietnam War, they want to insist that it was a good thing to fight against communism, that it was a good thing to bring an end to the Soviet Union. They want to keep those separate. They want to say, "That's something that happened later on."

But if communism was bad, then you can't say that the Japanese government who fought against communism was completely bad. It's because Japan lost that the People's Republic of China was founded and the Soviet Union survived. By the way, Mr. Abe is now on his way to Russia to speak with Putin tomorrow (January 22) over a peace treaty*, right? I'm aware of that. Anyway, if only Japan were a bit stronger, don't you think? Before the war (Pacific War) started, the Japanese-Soviet Non-aggression Pact was signed. If Japan weren't

---

* On January 21, 2019, Prime Minister Abe visited Moscow. The next day, on January 22, he and President Putin held talks regarding the Northern Territories and the signing of a peace treaty between Japan and Russia.

so weak, and they wreaked havoc on Russia from the rear, or Siberia, as General Nogi did, then the Soviets wouldn't have had the power to attack Germany. Hitler wouldn't have ended as he did.

So, it's quite complicated. They say the Northern Territories belong to Russia, but they're very sneaky. They haven't been taught to reflect on the fact that they were founded by demons. Roosevelt, Mao Zedong, and Stalin are the three demons, you know? In my eyes, they are a trio of demons.

Those three demons built the post-war, UN-centered permanent member system and led the world. They suppressed and virtually exploited the defeated countries, and doled out the money to the countries around the defeated. Mr. Trump may start the next war, but it would be considered new and separate from the past wars. So, to tell the truth, history needs to be rewritten. There was a war between Japan and the U.S., but I believe it was a war of hegemony, to put it positively.

The liberation of India was truly Japan's mission. If Japan hadn't acted, India wouldn't have been liberated, after all. Japan sank the British warships.* I'll say this because I'm from the U.K.; many of the British warships were made in Liverpool. Two of them were sunk completely, so the Indians were really happy.

From this, everyone became aware that being yellow does not mean being inferior, including the Filipinos and the Vietnamese. Everyone realized that. But the Americans wanted to continue to be the superheroes, so they made up their own myth. After the war, people slowly learned about the good and the bad sides of what Hitler did.

---

* The British battleship, Prince of Wales, which was considered the strongest in the world at the time, and the battle cruiser, Repulse, were sunk by Japanese aircraft on December 10, 1941, in the Naval Battle of Malaya.

Why were so many huge demons born in post-war societies?

JOHN LENNON

What the EU is doing now is forming something like the satellite countries of the former Soviet Union [*laughs*]. The EU gathered many economically challenged countries and is trying to extract money from the U.K., Germany, and France. That's the kind of group it is. So, the U.K. wants to drop out, but is having trouble because they would be bullied if they left Europe. It has become a country without sovereignty. The EU is in a predicament because it has no "master" right now. Just because people gather around doesn't mean things will go smoothly.

Post-war societies gave birth to quite a lot of huge demons. This means we needed to doubt whether the nature of WWII was good.

SHIO OKAWA

But I think Mr. Churchill was also guided from the heavenly world.

JOHN LENNON

Yeah. So, the heavenly world had no plans to destroy the U.K.

2

The Way of Thinking to Strengthen Your Influence

Pitiful are humans who do not believe in the power of God and the power of faith

SHIO OKAWA

There are some things Japan must also reflect on, but Japan couldn't afford to become like Thailand* in order for El Cantare to be born in Japan.

JOHN LENNON

Well, if the emperor had remained a god, then El Cantare would have been oppressed for sure.

---

* In Thailand, the royal family and the majority of the country's citizens are Buddhists (of the Theravada sect), and in some ways, this was taken advantage of in order to protect the king's rule. Ideas and opinions that express criticism against the royal system receive severe punishment. See "Conversations with the Devil of Thailand's Theravada Buddhism," held on November 17, 2018.

SHIO OKAWA

Probably. We would've had to become more advanced as a religion. It's true that there was some truth in the things that the Westerners said.

JOHN LENNON

But you can check up on that if you give it serious thought in terms of freedom, democracy, and faith. If justice meant for noble people born under special circumstances to rule their people under an autocracy, then there would be no freedom or democracy. As for faith, it would be an "artificial" one. So, of course there would be problems.

SHIO OKAWA

Japan didn't have faith in the form of worshiping the Creator, so this is the first time, thanks to Master Ryuho Okawa. In the Western world, there has been faith in the Creator thanks to figures like Jesus, but Japan didn't have anything like that, so now...

JOHN LENNON

I don't know whether "a Paul" will come from amongst you and do something sometime later, but seeing that Happy Science is in "a critical but stable condition," I think it's doing the bare minimum where it can sustain itself if it can get as many believers as it loses every year. To me, it looks like all they're thinking about is how to spend the money they can get from the same wallet. At this time, the disciples don't seem to have what it takes to expand the group by themselves. So really, the spirit of rock is what you need. And you must not go the wrong way with that.

SHIO OKAWA

What matters is which way rock works, right?

JOHN LENNON

But it's difficult. There are some types of rock that simply destroy the inside (of Happy Science).

SHIO OKAWA

But we need to destroy the common sense outside of us.

JOHN LENNON

Yup, yup, yup, yup. It's not enough to just destroy the inside. That's the difficult part. I feel bad for you all. The work that you guys do might end up being the whole work. You (Shio Okawa) are trying to have Master Okawa work as long as he possibly can, but the amount of time he works might be all there will be. The rest may simply become demolition work. The same can be said of the Beatles and Namie Amuro, now that they're done. All you can do is to bathe in their afterglow.

Oh, humans are pitiful. They don't believe in the true power of God or in the power of faith. They (disciples) have to gain more power, but it's easier said than done. They don't have confidence in themselves. That's the problem. Usually, movies and other means are used to expand a particular market, but the disciples make such activities a part of their routine work, and divide and assign that amongst themselves. So, I'm sorry to say, but that's different from us rock 'n' rollers.

You must spread the teachings to hundreds of millions of people

SHIO OKAWA

There are lyrics to music. Having lyrics means you can include some part of the Truth. Of course, you can express it in the melody, but since this is Happy Science, we shouldn't neglect that part. Rather, we should compromise the level of music a little and simply incorporate the Truth in each song. Then, it will become a bullet of light.

JOHN LENNON

The thing is, you can't be satisfied with just a thousand listeners. Ryuho Okawa's work must reach out to at least a hundred million people. Definitely.

SHIO OKAWA

Just to let you know, our latest movie, *The Laws of the Universe-Part I* had songs and lyrics composed by Master Okawa, and he really put a lot of effort into those five songs. People in other countries said that the music was very good, so I think our songs can make it in other countries.

JOHN LENNON

[*Sighs.*]

SHIO OKAWA

Or, I guess not?

JOHN LENNON

You know, you guys are saying that you've got as many moviegoers as you did fifteen years ago. You guys are probably thinking that the disciples are working hard all over the place, but unfortunately, most of them are red-tape. Considering that, sometimes I feel I should appreciate the fact that the Beatles had female fans screaming and running around the grounds.

SHIO OKAWA

But if you ask whether the Beatles songs will remain for thousands of years from now...

JOHN LENNON

Hmm.

SHIO OKAWA

The teachings of Jesus have been passed down for two thousand years.

JOHN LENNON

Hmm. I'd be happy just to have songs like "Power to the People," "Imagine," and "Let It Be," passed down because those are enough to convey our will. He (Master Okawa) is working diligently making things, but it's hard to appeal to the public based only on quantity.

SHIO OKAWA

Master Okawa is only trying to appeal to them by quantity because we are the only disciples he has.

JOHN LENNON

It's because all they say is, "I just can't do it." But if he has no one to receive his idea, he'll just find another way.

The fundamental issue is that Happy Science isn't expanding enough

SHIO OKAWA

Master Ryuho Okawa gives his all into everything he creates, but because each doesn't reach so many people, he's trying to spread Happy Science by producing many things.

JOHN LENNON

[*Sighs.*] That's where Japan is odd; things don't spread as much as you'd think. But sometimes there are people like us who start out from Liverpool and become known throughout the world. Maybe it's better not to think about that and rather just work solely on imagining (that you're spreading throughout the world).

SHIO OKAWA

OK.

JOHN LENNON

Master's doing quite a lot of work. So, the fundamental issue is that Happy Science isn't spreading enough. This is too sad. But the same thing can be said of two thousand years of Christian history. It's actually the same.

Islam also is in a terrible state, they are out of control, like a large herd of buffaloes running wild. Nothing can keep them under control. They are contrary to you guys. They are a mob. They are doing a lot of bad things everywhere. They are violating all kinds of human rights and clashing with other religions.

Even though Happy Science is making movies, it's hard for them to become the mainstream because about one thousand movies are released in Japan every year and they are all competing against each other. It's frustrating. But we in the spiritual world want to somehow come up with a way to spread the light. So, I hope that at least you guys can believe us.

SHIO OKAWA

I believe you. Even now, it gives me more energy just having you here.

JOHN LENNON

I can say my music isn't reaching far, but then the disciples explain the reason as "because it's not the real John Lennon." That's how they think.

SHIO OKAWA

I can see that they will think that way instead of thinking that they did poor work or did not promote well.

JOHN LENNON

They will probably say that if I were the real John Lennon, then my music should spread more. So, if they can't win the Academy Award, they will think something like, "We could've won it if the product itself was good. So, there's no reason why the International Headquarters needs to be active on this." Like that, everyone goes for the easy way out.

SHIO OKAWA
But I heard that there's quite a lot of lobbying going on at the Academy Awards.

JIMMU
I heard that you need to work on a lot of "politics."

JOHN LENNON
Yeah, yeah. That's something they haven't figured out yet.

SHIO OKAWA
And China is fighting to take over Hollywood now.

JOHN LENNON
There's a lot of Chinese money flowing in there now, but not so much from Japan.

SHIO OKAWA

That's true. Japanese people probably aren't interested in that at all.

JOHN LENNON

Well, it's an island country, after all.

Why were John Lennon and Paul McCartney born in the U.K.?

JOHN LENNON

The U.K. is also an island country, but was powerful enough to influence the world during its time of development. In our (the Beatles') days, we tried to come up with something that would light up the world, from the U.K., in the aftermath of WWII.

JINMU

After WWII, the U.K. declined and the U.S. took the lead.

JOHN LENNON

Declined, yeah.

JINMU

Why were you and Paul McCartney born in the U.K.?

JOHN LENNON

We were born during the war, when the U.K. was under attack. Before we were born, we had planned to contribute to post-war recovery. In Japan, there were people who did great work and inspired others after the war. The U.K. is considered a victorious country, but if we consider the battle between the U.K. and Germany, the truth is that the U.K. lost. France also lost. It's the U.S. and the Soviet Union that defeated Germany. We lost against Germany. The U.K. lost, France lost, and Germany was utterly defeated in the end. Berlin was destroyed. The EU is being run mainly by these three countries. So, right now the defeated countries of WWII are leading the group of small countries. And China and the U.S. are being nosy. Plus, there's Russia. Yeah.

There's something about New York that changes people

SHIO OKAWA
New York is a melting pot, and one of the cities that Master Ryuho Okawa is rather fond of. It's a city where freedom and fairness are expressed well.

JOHN LENNON
Yeah, there are the freedom to bear arms and the freedom to assassinate people.

SHIO OKAWA
It's true that there are such dangers.

JOHN LENNON

Forty-four percent of Americans live in a household owning a gun.

SHIO OKAWA

But it's interesting that the U.S., even though it has such a young history, was able to develop such cities. Though there aren't as many great figures, Americans were able to build high-level cities. Was the power of Jesus working on the U.S. through John Lennon?

JOHN LENNON

Hmm. We were "the forerunners of the space civilization" a bit.

SHIO OKAWA

Oh, really?

JOHN LENNON

We experimented to see if we could make development by mixing different things.

Immigrants are virtually coming into Japan right now, but Japan is reluctant to include an immigration policy. However, we were "ahead of the space age." We could spread more if we were active in the U.S. rather than the U.K. That way, we could spread our message to the world. We wanted to become big in the U.S., and I chose the U.S. as my resting place. I went to New York. There's something about New York that changes people. The Statue of Liberty has power. She's the "rock" part of the French Revolution. Yeah.

The state of mind of musicians who become involved with drugs

JINMU
Some people who like rock music do drugs like marijuana and narcotics. I think you also went through such a period.

JOHN LENNON

Yeah. I was like, "What's wrong with taking nude photos of myself?"

SHIO OKAWA

But after that, you did say you could talk about the danger of doing drugs, so you were kind of against it.

JOHN LENNON

[*Laughs.*] Well, I've been told many times that I was crazy, so I meant to say that drugs can do that to you.

JINMU

What do you think of that time, now that you're back in the heavenly world?

JOHN LENNON

Hmm... the police chasing us with a stick, they really did look like the demons in hell. There were things like alcohol and drugs that they found, yeah.

SHIO OKAWA

I think it's fine that you gained more and more fans because of your feverish activities, but on the other hand, you lost your freedom and...

JOHN LENNON

We gradually lost our freedom, and what's the word... "confined"?

SHIO OKAWA

You felt like you were confined?

JOHN LENNON

Yup, yup, yup, yup.

SHIO OKAWA

You had a mental breakdown, right?

JOHN LENNON

Yeah. So, I can't believe that you guys are able to take a stroll.

SHIO OKAWA

In a sense, we're fortunate to be in an environment where we can go for a walk.

JOHN LENNON

In a way, you've "given up." That's why the disciples are going along with that and taking it easy. I mean, if Happy Science becomes fanatical, you won't be able to walk around. Happy Science used to be like that too, at one time.

SHIO OKAWA

Oh, yes in the 1990s...

JOHN LENNON

Yeah, it was like that in the nineties. So, you withdrew to Utsunomiya at that time.[*] But the disciples now probably won't understand that. Probably not. But all you can do is to do what you can. Yeah. The disciples complain, say negative things, and obstruct things, so it might be better if you constantly open a path by yourselves or pool resources effectively on your own. Hmm.

The disciples have yet to practice "possibility thinking"

JOHN LENNON

This session alone is very tough, but Master's giving over a hundred lectures per year, so it's really hard for disciples. They can't remember

---

[*] To establish a long-lasting foundation for Happy Science, plans were made to build head temples as the core centers of Happy Science's faith. In August, 1996, the first head temple, Sohonzan Shoshinkan, opened in Utsunomiya City, and the Happy Science headquarters moved there temporarily to work on the early operations.

everything. They haven't studied enough to be able to teach others. Although they're busy with miscellaneous work, they need to study, but they can't remember. Master's writing a lot of books and other things in English, too. They have no idea what's going on. They're wondering as to what exactly Master is trying to do.

It's like working for a convenience store. They're basically saying that there's no way two employees can sell ten thousand or twenty thousand items. What they're saying is that two employees can sell or memorize at most about twenty items.

SHIO OKAWA
Convenience store employees have rather detailed and complicated work to do.

JOHN LENNON
Over ten thousand right? Items, I mean.

SHIO OKAWA

Yes. Convenience stores nowadays have everything, such as dry cleaning and delivery services. You can buy books there, too.

JOHN LENNON

Yeah, of course. You can pay your taxes, and do bank businesses too, like transferring and withdrawing money.

SHIO OKAWA

Yes. They have ATMs there and you can make deferred payments, too. They use the barcode to process it.

JOHN LENNON

Just two people do all that, right?

SHIO OKAWA

And more foreigners are working there.

JOHN LENNON

Yup, yup.

SHIO OKAWA

It's quite a lot of work [*laughs*].

JINMU

It's a lot of work, so not many Japanese people apply to work there anymore.

JOHN LENNON

That's the kind of complaints the disciples are making. What they're saying is, in terms of convenience stores, "Please make the job manageable for two people, to about twenty items." So, they've yet to practice "possibility thinking."

What the disciples, or "obstructionists" of Master Okawa, truly think

SHIO OKAWA

Besides, if one is aware that they're lacking in the power to spread the Truth, then they should at least try not to obstruct Master's work.

JOHN LENNON

Well, they aren't blocking, but they're protecting themselves.

SHIO OKAWA

Ah, to prevent themselves from falling apart?

JOHN LENNON

Yeah. Everyone is like that in a public office.

SHIO OKAWA

Then, maybe we can get the graduates of HSU (Happy Science University)* who are highly self-confident to do more and more work...

JOHN LENNON

Tell them to "rock." They don't have to go to the office. They don't have to be working in the workplace, just let them go out in the city. Hahaha [*laughs.*]

SHIO OKAWA

So, we should tell them, "Just spread, just convey the teachings"?

JOHN LENNON

Tell them not to enter the office. Yeah.

---

* Happy Science University is a private institution that began in April, 2015, in Japan, with the aim to explore human happiness and create a new civilization. There are two campuses—one in Chosei-mura in Chiba prefecture, and another one in Tokyo—and four departments of study: the Faculty of Human Happiness, the Faculty of Successful Management, the Faculty of Future Industry, and the Faculty of Future Creation.

"The Beatles is just a forerunner"

JOHN LENNON

Umm, I guess this session turned out a little odd.

SHIO OKAWA

We are very grateful to have you and (the guardian spirit of) Paul McCartney help us, but...

JOHN LENNON

Sorry, but I want to be honest and say we aren't receiving that much "welcoming" vibes. Okay?

SHIO OKAWA

I'm very sorry.

JOHN LENNON

The work... how do I say this? They're working like a snail. "Let us all study and think how escargot is cooked," something like that. Our lifespan is short, so if we don't do things when we can, we won't be able to do them at some point. At the time, you're the only "joint guarantor," but we never know if Master Okawa will work until ninety or one hundred. He has to work hard while he still can.

SHIO OKAWA

I mean, the Creator is giving us things and ways of thinking that He considers good in each field, so it will be a shame to the people of later generations if the present-day disciples don't at least receive them as they are. If we can do our best to receive them exactly as they were provided, then we can pass them down.

JOHN LENNON

They're all wearing suits and pretending to be salaried workers. [*About five seconds of silence pass.*] Well... maybe it's time to pass the baton to the next generation. Being unable to spread wider means that you've reached your limit. In the music industry, it would be like changing the singer, producer, company, or other things like that. But I guess it comes down to the fact that a single person cannot make so many changes. It's a pity, but we might have to rely on people who will live one thousand to two thousand years from now. Truthfully, the Beatles was nothing but a harbinger in terms of El Cantare's philosophies.

SHIO OKAWA
This may sound rude, but that is the truth.

JOHN LENNON
That's how it should look. But it doesn't.

SHIO OKAWA
The fact that the Beatles looks greater than Master Okawa indicates our poor level of awareness.

JOHN LENNON

The fact that we do not look like a harbinger. Yeah. That is what is lacking with the disciples. To them, Ryunosuke Akutagawa and Soseki Natsume look greater (than Master Okawa). So, they're actually degrading Master Okawa. I could say a lot, but this (spiritual interview) won't do much good because internal criticism won't be published externally to the public. That's the type of organization Happy Science is.

SHIO OKAWA

No, don't worry. Recently, we've been disclosing such things too.

JOHN LENNON

So, Happy Science now has a "masochistic view of its history" then? I see.

JINMU

As a material to encourage self-transformation.

SHIO OKAWA

Right. Otherwise, we'll be a disgrace to our believers.

JOHN LENNON

Well... it's a pity. But you guys live longer than I did, so I guess that makes up for it.

Happy Science needs people like Shoin Yoshida and Jan Hus who take action

JOHN LENNON

Eventually, a complete stranger will be working hard to spread the teachings, like Paul, who did not know Jesus. People who you don't even know will appear and spread the word.

SHIO OKAWA

Mr. Junta Sato* also said something similar.

---

* Junta Sato was a former teacher of Shoichi Watanabe. See "The Spiritual Message from Junta Sato" held on November 11, 2017.

JOHN LENNON

Yeah. I think so. People who are actually getting paid won't be like that. People who aren't getting paid will do it. That's what I think. The purpose of your world missionary work might be to find such people.

SHIO OKAWA

Well, someone in Hong Kong or elsewhere who is listening to Master may take action.

JOHN LENNON

Yeah. You need someone like Shoin Yoshida or Jan Hus.*

---

* Jan Hus (around 1370–1415) was a religious thinker and reformer from Bohemia who became the head and preacher of Prague's Bethlehem Chapel, and he also served as a dean at the University of Prague. Through such works as translating the Bible into the Czech language, he devoted much effort toward the education of his people. But as a result of his criticism against the Roman church and his work toward religious reform, he was charged of heresy and burned at the stake.

Make Happy Science an organization that spreads wide like an amoeba, not vertically long

JOHN LENNON

I don't think people on the inside can do anything. It may be better not to make the inside any larger because it will become "a public office" and the people in it will think only about trying to maintain that. "An achievement of 100 percent every year" will mean "100 percent compared to the year before." They won't do more than that, so maybe you'll have to have someone outside do it. You might have to give up on certain things. As for your movies, we sometimes help you, but it feels like we are doing the same thing every time, so we are a bit sad about that. You haven't made a breakthrough, so I feel that you don't rock enough. Rock in your nature, I mean.

SHIO OKAWA

But we, disciples have much smaller and dimmer light compared to Master Okawa or Jesus, so we shouldn't try to add value by ourselves. Rather, what is asked of us is how much of Master Okawa's intention we can understand, which I feel adds more value.

JOHN LENNON

[*About five seconds of silence pass.*] Uh, it means disciples aren't as capable as convenience store workers. Convenience store workers are the popular thing right now. Hmm. It's tough. I don't know where they will pop up, but those kinds of people will appear. It's really... You know, you should avoid making Happy Science an organization that is vertically long. Avoid that as much as you can. You should make it an organization that will spread wide like an amoeba. It's better not to make an organization that requires a lot of approvals. Yeah. That's why you would want to use younger people, but in the end, they can't offer the level of work they're expected to do and fall apart. No matter how many of them you try to use, they fail.

SHIO OKAWA

Exactly. In the end, just because you're young doesn't necessarily mean you can rock. Rather, you need to destroy the inside...

JOHN LENNON

They destroy the inside, but end up falling apart themselves before being able to spread to the people outside. That's how it is.

What matters is that people become impressed by you and follow you

SHIO OKAWA

And if you get promoted to a high position, you tend to preserve yourself.

JOHN LENNON

I mean, one of your sons served as the Vice-Chairperson (in Happy Science) and he's saying to give him everything, but if he were so capable, he should be able to do the same work outside, too. However, he can't.

SHIO OKAWA

I can understand well that he would become a bit crazy if he were like the Beatles, who has zealous fans all over the world. But if he isn't even close to that level, he would be wrong to think that his position was gained by his work alone.

JOHN LENNON

Yeah, yeah. Even the writers who have received the Naoki Prize, many of them actually live with the bare minimum, making just enough money to survive. So, it's wrong for people who haven't reached that level to think that they're geniuses. It's the results that matter, you know? How many people are impressed by you and follow you? That's everything.

SHIO OKAWA

When you think you're the best, you won't be able to accept the thoughts of others who help you. That's what you mean, right?

The overwhelming difference between Master and his disciples: the case of a lecturer's seminar in Thailand

JOHN LENNON

There was a report from Thailand earlier (on a seminar). The staff there rented a hotel room, showed Master's English lecture ("What is 'Truth?'" on a DVD), had a movie screening, and provided a meal. It was a small scale event, but the disciples were doing it with everything they had. This really shows how hard they are making it for Master to hold an event. You can really see that Happy Science will go bust if Master were to leave things in disciples' hands completely. If screening a movie and a Master's lecture can only attract as few as that, then there would be even less of an audience if a movie and a lecture weren't shown. Even if they rented a hotel that can fit one thousand people, only a handful will show up. That's all they can do. So, the reality is really tough. It can't be helped. The difference is what makes a star. That's how it is. For example, in the case of Namie Amuro, there would be no major dome tours without her. Others can't do what she did.

SHIO OKAWA

Yes. Though there are many backup dancers...

JOHN LENNON

There are many of them, and they have a lot of

songs, too. But they can't do it, right? That's what you call talent. It can't be helped.

Keep trying hard, at least for fifty years, hoping that Happy Science will eventually spread wider

JOHN LENNON

In my eyes, I can say that you're doing a good job, but please work hard for fifty years. If you keep working, it will lead to trust, and though you might not expand, you can build a firm foundation. Happy Science might break up into different groups later on, but in the end, you might spread wider somehow. It might split up into many small sects, and if these sects hold their activities in different places, that might lead to your spreading wider, actually. Maybe that's how it should be.

Even though you're opening branches and main temples, you're not creating new members around there and turning those towns into "temple towns," right? That's not good. If Master were to reveal himself 100 percent to the public, then he wouldn't have a suitable place to live. He won't be able to go anywhere. Yeah. He's like us. If he lived in an apartment, he would be shot. That's who he is. Disciples wouldn't be shot, no matter how much they appear to the public. Yeah. Haha [*laughs*]. Sorry for sounding grouchy and being unproductive today.

SHIO OKAWA
Thank you very much.

CHAPTER THREE

His Message to All the People

John Lennon's Spiritual Message Part 3

*Originally recorded in Japanese on January 23, 2019,
in the General Headquarters of Happy Science in Japan,
and later translated into English.*

Interviewers from Happy Science[*]

Hisaaki Takeuchi

Executive Director of Happy Science
  in Charge of Media and Culture Division

Senior Managing Director of ARI Production Co., Ltd.
  Overseeing the Area of Entertainment

Akitoshi Nakata

Director General in Charge of the Entertainment,
  Performing, and Media Arts Course of the Faculty of Future
  Creation of Happy Science University

Director General (in Charge of Music) of the Media and Culture
  Division of Happy Science

Director of ARI Production Co., Ltd.

Kazuhiro Ichikawa

Senior Managing Director of Happy Science

Chief Director of International Headquarters

*The opinions of the spirit do not necessarily reflect those of Happy Science Group.
For the mechanism behind spiritual messages, see the end section.*

---

[*] Interviewers are listed in the order that they appear in the transcript.
Their professional titles represent their positions at the time of the interview.

1

The "Rock" Way of Life that Led to Breaking Through the Times

Travels in Japan and India led to changes in John Lennon

RYUHO OKAWA

Today[*], I would like to record a formal version of John Lennon's spiritual message. Because he is already a legend, some people might have only a vague idea of who he was. So, let me tell you a bit about him.

John Lennon was the leader and main vocalist of the famous band, the Beatles. He was born in Liverpool, England, in 1940. In 1960, at about age twenty, he formed the Beatles band. They made a big breakthrough from 1962 to about 1964, and

---

[*] January 23, 2019.

became famous worldwide. In America, their concerts were held inside baseball stadiums, but because of their huge popularity, they started needing heavy security, and eventually, they stopped performing. I think that they were the first to use baseball stadiums as concert venues. Elvis Presley's time came a bit before theirs, and it seems he inspired them to take interest in rock music.

When it comes to their family, it is a bit complicated.

Only John Lennon, their leader, was assassinated in 1980, at the age of forty. The band's active years lasted from about 1962 to 1969, but their activity ended completely by about the year 1970. Before this, John Lennon became married to Yoko Ono, but his distance between the other members grew even further since then. In him a growing interest in Japan developed, and he seemed to begin having a bit of a strange character after he went to India. His activities took on a more political and religious tone since his marriage, and his sense of "love and peace" probably grew stronger around that time.

And the Beatles disbanded in 1970. And Yoko Ono miscarried around three times. They must have gone through a lot, and when Sean was born, John Lennon retired from music activity, and for five years or so, he became a househusband to be able to raise Sean and to take care of the housework. When Sean was about the age of five, John Lennon felt that it was time and began to work on his music again. He recorded an album and a single that got released in November, 1980.

However, on December 8, he was shot and killed in front of his apartment. Historically, this was the day of America's declaration of war with Japan, and this same day, in later years, also became the day that the Buddha reborn conquered the Devil and attained enlightenment.

John Lennon was living in the Dakota Apartments in Manhattan, New York. Those in the know will remember how the classic horror film depicting the birth of the Devil's baby, *Rosemary's Baby**, had been filmed there. It's interesting, but he purchased and chose such a place to be his home and it also became the place where he faced assassination. I don't know what to make of these events. I'm not sure if John Lennon had a liking for such things, but I have seen this building before. John Lennon was assassinated in December 1980, and in the summer of 1982, the trading company I was working for transferred me to the United States, so he was assassinated about a year and a half before I was there. Maybe there are many hidden secrets regarding this. He and I were about sixteen years apart when he was alive, and I rather regret not taking much interest in him while he was still alive, knowing we were living in the same times together.

---

* *Rosemary's Baby*, directed by Roman Polanski (1968; the United States: Paramount Pictures).

John Lennon was eccentric, and practical work was not his strength

RYUHO OKAWA

At Happy Science, we have a series of English study materials called the *Kuro-Obi Eigo E No Michi** (lit. "The Road to Black Belt in English"), a ten-volume series created prior to the *Kuro-Obi Eigo Shodan†* series (lit. "First-Degree Black Belt in English"). At the end of that series' sixth volume, there is a section titled, "A Collection of English by the Beatles," which has over thirty pages of quotes from them. If you feel it is cumbersome to learn everything about them, just read this section, and you can learn the main points from their statements. For example, you'll see the Japanese translation of the quote,

---

* See Ryuho Okawa, *Kuro-Obi Eigo E No Michi* [The Road to Black Belt in English] (Tokyo: Happy Science, 2012).

† See Ryuho Okawa, *Kuro-Obi Eigo Shodan* [First-Degree Black Belt in English] (Tokyo: Happy Science, 2013).

"Rock 'n' roll meant it was real; everything else was unreal.–John Lennon," and the English version of this quote, so if you skim through all of them, you will be able to know what kind of thinking they had. Paul McCartney was a Beatle's member who wrote the songs and lyrics like John Lennon did, and he is still living. Just recently, he held concerts at the Tokyo Dome,* at the age of seventy-six, so he has spent a long time spreading "the Beatles spirit."

John Lennon's soul is exactly how you would imagine it to be. He is eccentric, and anyone working with him will have a bit of a hard time. I don't think that his strengths are in management or in practical work, and he probably likes unique things. Many artists are like that. This side of him became more obvious after his marriage to Yoko Ono, who was also an eccentric person, and so, he was slightly disliked by other people in

---

* He held concerts at Tokyo Dome on October 31 and November 1, 2018.

the later years of his life, including by the other members of his band.

As you heard in the song, "Power to the People," earlier,* a political tone grew that resonated with the antiwar movement against the Vietnam War, so President Nixon used John's U.K. arrest for drug possession as a reason to stop John's re-entry into the United States. The FBI also wiretapped him and kept a watch on him. He even took this to court.† In the end, he passed away in the United States.

In that way, I feel John Lennon was not the type to systematically succeed, but the type who would rock the world by breaking through the times. That's my thought on him.

---

* "Power to the People" was playing in the background at the start of this recording.

† John Lennon was banned from re-entering the United States, but fought in court, and eventually was granted permanent residency in the United States.

The spirit of John Lennon is summoned

RYUHO OKAWA

For everyone's convenience, we will speak in Japanese for this spiritual message today. John Lennon did study Japanese while he was living. He practiced it with Yoko Ono at his side, so it makes me think sometimes that he might have thought he would need it later on when giving spiritual messages.

His soul seems to be closely related with Jesus Christ,* and I received Jesus' first spiritual message in June, 1981, six months after John Lennon's assassination. Though the souls of Jesus and John Lennon are not completely the same, John Lennon is very similar to the "rock aspect" of Jesus.

Let's let the interviewers freely interview him, then. This is a rare opportunity, so we should

---

* See chapter one of this book.

193

try not to ask him too many questions regarding Happy Science's inner affairs, and try to let him speak his thoughts on various topics. Now, we will start the spiritual message from John Lennon.

[*Closes his eyes and puts his hands together in prayer.*] John Lennon, the former main vocalist for the Beatles, I ask you to please come down to Happy Science General Headquarters [*claps once*] and give us your spiritual message.

[*Approximately ten seconds of silence pass.*]

2

Music Becomes Politically Influential as It Spreads Widely

"Now is the time, it feels like."

JOHN LENNON

Yes.

TAKEUCHI

Hello. I'm sure there are many people around the world who want to hear your message. Thank you for this precious opportunity today.

JOHN LENNON

Will people all over the world hear my message?

TAKEUCHI

Of course. Yes.

JOHN LENNON

It's not something you should promise me lightly, you know. To your people, "people all over the world" means just a sprinkling of them, doesn't it?

TAKEUCHI

No, that's not the case.

JOHN LENNON

Hmmm. Really? Isn't my message going to be heard by the Japanese people?

TAKEUCHI

Of course it will be heard by the Japanese people, but many Happy Science books can also be bought online in other countries.

JOHN LENNON

Hmm. Well, okay then…

TAKEUCHI

This spiritual message from you is the first official version in the world that we'll receive after your death. Could we…

JOHN LENNON

These days, I've been visiting (Master Okawa) often, especially since the new year started.

TAKEUCHI

Yes. Thank you very much.

JOHN LENNON

Now is the time, it feels like. That's my feeling.

> **"I wasn't trying to destroy anything.
> I was just being natural."**

TAKEUCHI

When we think of the Beatles band, you were

at the beginning of, and were the forerunners of, rock 'n' roll music. This music tears down the common sense of the world, not purely for destruction's sake, but to allow new creations. It promotes new values that the music incorporates. So, first, could I ask you about your image of rock music? Since your return to the spirit world, did your image of rock music change?

JOHN LENNON

I'm wondering if I ever destroyed anything. I wasn't trying to destroy anything. I was just being natural.

TAKEUCHI

I see.

JOHN LENNON

In living naturally and truthfully to myself, I was only speaking my honest feelings. People get tied down by the rules, cultures, and common sense values of the world, in addition to other such things, but I was just following my feelings and what felt the most natural and normal to me, that's all. So there was never any intent to destroy.

"Let It Be" was a song of desperation

TAKEUCHI

In the same vein of what you just said, your song, "Let It Be," was about being just as we are.

JOHN LENNON

That song was actually a song of desperation.

TAKEUCHI

A song of desperation [*laughs*]?

JOHN LENNON

That was a song of despair-about disbanding (the Beatles) [*laughs*].

TAKEUCHI

It's my favorite song. You mentioned right now about being natural, and in the world of the arts, such as in songs, music, and movies, I feel that letting yourself be as you are is a very important foundation.

JOHN LENNON

Is it "natural" to "let yourself be as you are"? Hmm, I don't know. If Master Okawa starts to sing "Let It Be," Happy Science might get disbanded, so you should be careful [*laughs*].

TAKEUCHI

Really [*smiles wryly*]?

JOHN LENNON

The end will be near. You should watch out for "Let It Be" because it will mean that things are beyond control.

TAKEUCHI
Oh, I see.

JOHN LENNON
If he says "let it be" to you, then that would mean you're not doing well, so you should really watch out.

TAKEUCHI
I understand [*smiles wryly*].

Being "the self exactly as God had originally created you" is rock

TAKEUCHI
What does letting it be, or being natural, mean to you?

JOHN LENNON
Well, is there a reason to wear clothes? Do you

see? Is photographing ourselves naked wrong? Do you see?

TAKEUCHI
Okay.

JOHN LENNON
Don't those questions trouble you? Being people in a religious organization, these questions can be troubling to you.

God gave Adam and Even His blessings because they had nothing to hide about, but when there was something to hide, He expelled them from the Garden of Eden. So putting on clothes wasn't what God wished us to do. Do you see? It was averse to Him.

So hiding yourself is an act that's undesirable or, said another way, acts of making yourself look better isn't desirable. Being more of your natural self, the self with nothing wrong in it and is exactly as God had originally created you. This is rock.

TAKEUCHI
Hmm.

JOHN LENNON
You have to remember yourself as you lived in the Garden of Eden. If you see an approaching serpent, then cook it and eat it. It's kind of like that.

TAKEUCHI
[*Laughs*] I see. From God's view, what is the most natural John Lennon like?

JOHN LENNON
I wouldn't know the answer to that. You would have to ask God about that.

TAKEUCHI
[*Smiles wryly*] Okay.

JOHN LENNON
Yeah.

TAKEUCHI

As Master Okawa said regarding you earlier on, you've gone back to the world of gods in the other world.

JOHN LENNON

I heard that Happy Science defines rock music as being close to hellish music.

TAKEUCHI

Really? [*Laughs in surprise*] Something like that's been...

JOHN LENNON

That notion is being broken through recently, but rumors said that about 10 percent of it is heavenly, and 90 percent of it is hellish. It made it very troublesome to me, because it was so difficult to come here (to Happy Science). So I had to say, "If you want to make another movie like *Rosemary's Baby*, I'd help you write the song for it."

TAKEUCHI
[*Laughs.*]

JOHN LENNON
Well it's like that.

The Beatles was not carefree. They had their freedom taken away from them.

TAKEUCHI
I could see while watching the interviews of the four of you and other past videos that everyone is extremely carefree and "letting themselves be" so to say...

JOHN LENNON

We were far from being carefree. What... We needed to be transported by police wagons, so we were, in no way, living in a carefree way.

TAKEUCHI

Well, that's true [*laughs*].

JOHN LENNON

Mr. Ryuho Okawa is definitely much more carefree than us. Our freedom got taken away when our female fans in the baseball stadium concerts, from the young to the slightly older [*laughs*], started screaming wildly.

Mr. Ryuho Okawa would also be able to gather people in a baseball stadium but because there is no one screaming, it's still safe for him. You should be careful when you start finding screaming fans in his audience; it could mean the end.

TAKEUCHI

During your time... Take Michael Jackson. He appeared a little later, but there were women fainting...

JOHN LENNON

Maybe if it were you, you would make (women) faint.

TAKEUCHI

Hm?

JOHN LENNON

Yeah, you might be able to. If you ever hold a live concert, I think women would faint.

TAKEUCHI

Really? [*Smiles wryly*] Music created by the Beatles has a sense of freedom and creativity, a sense of destruction, so...

JOHN LENNON

Actually, we weren't destroying anything at all. We thought of ourselves to be well-behaved, but the people around us didn't think so, that's all.

"Our scale exceeded what humans could accept."

TAKEUCHI

How was this kind of success created, the greatness of the Beatles?

JOHN LENNON

Our scale exceeded what humans could accept. It really was just that. While we were growing in popularity, we were welcomed everywhere. Everywhere we went, lots of people gathered, and we were welcomed.

But when we started to perform at baseball stadiums, our fans started to run out from their seats. So the police had to chase after them and catch them. As I was performing they started to "race," and that being dangerous, the policemen became irritated.

Even when we went to Japan, the security was extremely tight. We didn't know that the right-wing groups hated us so much. We weren't told about that. So, we were wondering why there was such tight security. And, in the end, we felt like we were moving around in police wagons. It wasn't safe to be anywhere.

This was why I bought the house in *Rosemary's Baby*, the house that you mentioned earlier, hoping that doing so would stop people from coming near me.

TAKEUCHI
I see.

"We wanted to unite the world as one through music"

JOHN LENNON

[*Speaking to Nakata*] You're from our generation, right?

NAKATA

[*Laughs*] Yes, I am. I would like to continue asking you questions about music. In your previous spiritual message*, you told us that you are a branch spirit of Jesus Christ, but you also taught us the immense mission of the Happy Science Group's movies and music. Thank you for letting us have another opportunity today.

JOHN LENNON

Yes. Yes.

---

* See chapter one of this book.

NAKATA

If you could explain the significance of your music, I'd be very grateful.

JOHN LENNON

Well, it's a strange thing. We wanted to unite the world as one through music. I especially wanted that to happen, but when music spreads widely, it also gains political influence. It doesn't possess any authoritative power, but it becomes a kind of authority, an influence.

As you mentioned in the introduction, President Nixon saw us as a crisis management case, and kept a close watch on us, especially on me. And if, for example, a political statement was made, (he was worried about) the possibility I could become involved in the Vietnam War. There were things like that.

For example, during the 9/11 attacks... was that in 2001? When the terrorist attacks happened, broadcasting stations were asked to refrain from playing my songs on a voluntary basis because they thought it would take away the will to fight. They felt that after the passenger planes hit the World Trade Center and thousands of people died, (hearing my songs) would sound like a message to do nothing. Things like that have happened, so when large political powers want to fight, my songs seem to get in their way regardless of the generation.

But then, we were neither communists. In countries such as China, the former Soviet Union, North Korea, and South Korea, it was very hard to penetrate their borders. Our music was banned from being listened to in those places, and we were not allowed to perform in those countries either, so we were clearly seen as their enemy. They knew that if we could do that, their regime would collapse.

So their regime would see collapse, but the western side also... how do I say this, the countries where an undemocratic person of power was acting single-handedly could see that our music had destructive powers against them as well. Well, so...maybe JFK's and John Lennon's assassinations were similar.

3

What Really Happened That Day on December 8, 1980

Was his assassination one man's fault, or was there also an organization?

TAKEUCHI

Because you mentioned about the assassination, I'd like to ask you about that.

JOHN LENNON

Okay.

TAKEUCHI

There continue to be many speculations from around the world about your assassination. Some say it was a CIA conspiracy, a KKK (the White supremacist group Ku Klux Klan) conspiracy, or that it was a fanatical fan, but looking back on that, now, in 2019, what do you see?

JOHN LENNON

Well the gun was fired five times. Yeah. There were about three shots that hit me, I think. He aimed for Yoko Ono but missed. It seems she had a bullet-proof aura. So, I, who was defenseless, was taken down. Firing five shots means that he must've had a real intent to kill.

TAKEUCHI

Yes.

JOHN LENNON

So, he had the clear intent to kill. He didn't even try to escape. He waited there until the police arrived. So, I'm sure he deliberately shot me.

TAKEUCHI

The killer's name was Mark Chapman, and do you think that there was an organization behind...

JOHN LENNON

I think there was. Well, there is the KKK, and

there was probably an American conservative group, too. He seemed to be a Presbyterian. I think he was someone who felt saved by the Beatles, and things turned for the worse again afterwards. Well, of course the Devil's organization could have helped him as well.

But overall, I was not destined to live a long life. That was my destiny. Attractive men die faster, people like you and me. The not-so-great-ones live longer. Sorry about that. Forgive me if I offended anyone.

So attractive men die faster. It's great that Master Ryuho Okawa is living longer. It really is.

He sensed he was in danger since the 1960s

TAKEUCHI
When you looked back on that, you said that it was your destiny, but was there a divine plan behind that, or was it purely an accidental thing?

JOHN LENNON

I sensed danger to myself since a long while back, even since the 1960s. Initially I was just a kid. So, when many people were screaming for us, and the baseball stadiums became full wherever we went, I was just happy. Simply happy. But afterwards there were crisis management issues... If you've never been in danger by being out in public, it's probably hard to imagine what it feels like to be in those circumstances. And it was like that for the longest time. With crowds of fifty thousand or so people gathering, no one could guarantee that a crazy person would not be among them.

Master Ryuho Okawa has been through experiences like that (when he gave lectures) at the Tokyo Dome, eleven times. So, he knows. Was it about twenty-four years ago that he spoke at the Tokyo Dome the last time (in the 1990s)? I think he spoke twice in the year 1995—once in summer, and once in winter.

He was warned several times by the police to stop (the lecture) at the Tokyo Dome. The Aum incident (the subway sarin gas attack in Tokyo) had just happened in March. And (Happy Science) was voicing criticism against the Aum religious group. If they carried in a bomb and detonated it inside the stadium, the damage would have been uncontrollable. And that is why Happy Science set up metal detectors at the entrances, but bombs are not always metal. They can be aqueous bombs and there are also plastic bombs that can't be detected. So even the police said that it would be impossible to guard a location like the Tokyo Dome, and asked him to please stop the event at both the Yokohama Arena and the Tokyo Dome. But Master Okawa is strong, and being asked to cancel it only further strengthened his determination to go through with it. He thought, "If they want to assassinate me, then they can try" and actually did not cancel the event.

But after a year, he "went underground" for about ten years, when he realized it will be unwise to keep going. I also "went underground" to raise my child. I spent about five years to do that. And if you also include the years prior to that, I went underground for about nine years in total without any music activity. And when I finally emerged nine years later, I was assassinated [*laughs*].

So being too popular is not a good thing, either. To be steadily popular, is the best, probably. If your popularity explodes... I think you wanted to ask me about the secret to our widespread popularity, but not having popularity can also lead to longevity, so that is also a good thing. If your popularity explodes around the world, or in your country, you will always have a crazy person who will come out of that. I think Master Okawa couldn't easily walk around Tokyo in the 1990s.

He was not intending to destroy anything, but only singing from his heart

TAKEUCHI

After rising to fame, you stepped back and became a househusband, but did you kind of foresee that you'd be assassinated, the way that President Lincoln had foreseen it?

JOHN LENNON

The American government saw me as a crisis management case. Nixon's administration wanted to evict me from the United States. So I wouldn't be surprised if I was a government target. It seemed like I was being wiretapped and whenever I opened the door to leave my apartment, there was always a man in black standing there just across the street. And they would follow our car around. It was the FBI. They were basically saying, "We are openly keeping you under observation."

They were pressuring me to avoid making political statements on the radio and television and at my performances, right? Because of the ongoing Vietnam War, my music sounded like an antiwar movement, so they tried to prevent people from listening to it. But I didn't have any intent to destroy anything. I was simply singing from my heart.

4

Music, Life, His Genius, and Madness

When you become popular and huge, you will also go through many unpleasant things

TAKEUCHI
You married Yoko Ono, and since then, you began to voice political ideas more strongly.

JOHN LENNON
Yeah.

TAKEUCHI
You sang in "Imagine" about creating world peace and the world becoming united as one. And I want to ask you, what was happening during this turning point in your philosophy?

JOHN LENNON

All things start to have political influence when they become huge. So as long as you are small and never become a huge hit, then you'll work as a musician all through your life, and that will be it.

There were times I received huge sums of wealth, which was rare, but people would then say to me, "Let me manage your wealth." At the point that people start coming to you to set up a company and manage it for you, disputes will start. Lawsuits will increase, too.

As you become huge, you will also have to go through various unpleasant things as that. So, it's better to be small sometimes, but I wonder why we became so huge. I guess, hmm, that maybe it was the sin of our youth. We just tried to go as far as we could, all the way. And there were aspects of doing that that were good, but when considering that our activity lasted only several years, there could have been a different way of doing it, too.

At first, we were trying to be cool. After all, being cool was the start of rock music and was what the younger generations admired. So we were trying to be cool, to be loved, and to be popular, and we didn't know that we would end up that way. It might be the same as hurting your shoulder while doing your best in every pitch you throw.

You are doing a good job. I mean you are stopping things just on the verge of getting popular, right? All of it. You are stopping all of it, right before getting there, right?

TAKEUCHI
Actually, it's not like that at all [*laughs wryly*].

JOHN LENNON
You're doing incredible. Your way of "stopping"

things is just beautiful. It's just incredible. Your political party... if you had succeeded at getting elected into one hundred seats at the outset, you would have been assassinated. No one was assassinated because you weren't elected into any seats. Your movies don't explode into popularity either, and so you're able to create more of them each year. That's truly incredible. That is the secret to winning in life. Yeah.

He was born "to heal the devastation in Europe and other areas of the world" through his music

ICHIKAWA

You just mentioned the sin of youth and the wish to be cool...

JOHN LENNON

Hm? Oh! You were here.

ICHIKAWA

Yes. I'm sorry [*laughs*] [*the audience laughs*]. Right now, I feel the sparkle of your soul, and, could I ask you what self-sacrifice means to you?

JOHN LENNON

Well, that's something I never thought about. That was just something that never crossed my mind. Never.

ICHIKAWA

So you lived the way your soul wanted to, that's all?

JOHN LENNON

Hmm. That was just something I never thought about. I never thought about self-sacrifice. I only thought about working myself to the fullest, and just putting my everything into things. Other than that, I knew that when my fuel became empty, I would need to slow down.

ICHIKAWA

But there are many people in the world who feel a sense of mission, but aren't able to fulfill their mission to their fullest. If we could, could we have your advice regarding putting our all into our lives?

JOHN LENNON

Well, I'm able to let most things slide. But I can't forgive the people who speak badly about Paul McCartney and those who say that Yoko Ono is ugly. These two types of people are the people I cannot forgive. I can forgive most things other than that. Yeah.

NAKATA

We'd like to hear more about Paul McCartney and Yoko Ono later on, but there are questions I'd like to ask you about the period before the Beatles was formed...

JOHN LENNON

Oh, before the band formed.

NAKATA

Yes. I heard that you were born in Liverpool, England, a seaport.

JOHN LENNON

Yeah, I was.

NAKATA

I hear it was a small town, and from there, you went to London and also went on to "conquer" the United States.

JOHN LENNON

Yeah, yes.

NAKATA

When you came down to Earth from Heaven, did you choose London, England, for its appeal as a cultural center? And what was it like in comparison to New York?

JOHN LENNON
Well, London was scary.

NAKATA
I see.

JOHN LENNON
Yes. So I thought of starting from the countryside. And there was also a war going on at that time.

NAKATA
Right.

JOHN LENNON
It was also very possible we would lose the war. I was born in 1940, you know? The war started in 1939, so Germany was very scary to us. There was fear that we would be crushed, and we knew

about the possibility of losing. I mean my middle name was "Winston*"...I'm "John Winston Lennon," so I think that my parents had feelings about that.

So it's true that I was born with the postwar reconstruction in mind. I wanted to give post-war England their courage. I was born to heal the devastation in Europe and other areas of the world through my music.

NAKATA

And under that kind of circumstance, you went to Hamburg, Germany, before debuting...

JOHN LENNON

Ah, yeah, yeah. Yeah we went there.

NAKATA

I heard that you performed throughout the night, and went through a period of building

---

* John Lennon's middle name, Winston, was named after Winston Churchill.

up your experience in this way. Could you say that this was a very important step? That your success was a result of your efforts?

JOHN LENNON

Hmmm... I'm not sure if you could call it a period of building up experience. Hamburg was not a good place for high-schoolers to go to [*laughs*]. It was a city for having fun. Many Japanese people right now don't have this image of Hamburg, but when we were high school kids, if you heard we're going to Hamburg to perform, this meant that we're probably going there for mischief. I feel bad about saying this, but the city of Sodom and Gomorrah was the image that people had of that city. It was a bit of a spreeing town. And if you went there, you wouldn't want to spend your time studying. But I think we were received well there anyway.

I don't know if you could call it accumulating experience, but we were hoping to gain a little confidence. It was that kind of a step for us.

It let us see that we'd be accepted by German audiences, too. Germany, also… It was the post-war period in Germany, after being defeated, and there was still animosity between the U.K. and Germany. So if we could expand British music into Germany, that would help the reconciliation between our countries make more progress, including between the people of both countries. Maybe it was audacious of us to think so, but that was what we wanted to do.

Genius and madness coexist

ICHIKAWA

I heard that when you were twelve years old, you thought that you were a genius.

JOHN LENNON

No, no, don't mention things like that [*laughs*].

ICHIKAWA

No, no, I think it's incredible.

JOHN LENNON

Why are you saying something that you don't need to mention [*audience laughs*], something that might get me assassinated again?

ICHIKAWA

But afterwards, you said that genius and madness are but a hairbreadth from each other...

JOHN LENNON

Isn't that something that's often said, in general? It has nothing to do with me.

ICHIKAWA

Could I ask you about what separates a genius and a madman?

JOHN LENNON

Well, that is...Am I being blamed for this? Is it that?

ICHIKAWA

No, of course not. I wanted to ask you about what you were really trying to say...

JOHN LENNON

The saying that genius and madness are but a hairbreadth from each other is heard often, so it's not that... well...Maybe they're not a hairbreadth from each other, maybe they are coexisting. We shouldn't say it's "a hairbreadth," we should say that they "are one."

ICHIKAWA

There are people who are not accepted by society and are alone, even though they see themselves as geniuses.

JOHN LENNON

Hmm. Maybe you have to be a little out of sync with the times to be a genius. People who go with the times are good at living their lives. So, people who are adaptable to that degree are probably making efforts, but it might be a bit difficult to become geniuses. But they have the possibility to achieve success.

The kind of success that we saw was, how do I describe it, [*laughs*] like a zero fighter plane dive-bombing, and then, once it succeeds, it plummets to its own death. So they are probably different things. It really is a hairbreadth. It's having the sense that people dying means you are also dying. It's a bit like that. I mean, I lived a long time after that, until I was forty. It was a long time, even if my life continued only until I was forty years old. My job had finished at age thirty, so it would have been alright if that was the age I died at.

But even though it was only several years, I am really happy I was able to capture the hearts of many people around the world and give them messages. Since I started to sense personal danger to myself when my political aspect started to come out, I think I couldn't have escaped it completely, either way. And our activities included the problem of world peace as one issue, but another issue was the racial problem. This was something Yoko and I were especially thinking about.

When we performed in America, we said that it's ridiculous to separate the white people and black people in restrooms and where they were allowed to sit. Even though we were still young men and could have seemed cheeky, we said, "The Americans are still doing this? Wow, how behind the times you are." We said something like that. Because things like that didn't happen in the U.K. To totally segregate the black people and the white people in the restaurants, the restrooms, the buses, and at the concerts was something that did not happen in the U.K. Definitely not.

This was being carried on in America just as a matter of fact thing. While we were active in the sixties, the black liberation movement was really progressing. Martin Luther King, Jr. was assassinated and other people were also assassinated, and we were in the same period. It was also during the racial liberation movement.

John Lennon's view of Japan

JOHN LENNON

Showing openly that I moved to the United States and was married to a Japanese person there might have seemed to people who fought in the war as if I was being spiteful.

I think you will be going to Hiroshima[*] or some place, soon. Is it this week? The reason they were able to drop atomic bombs onto Hiroshima

---

[*] On January 26, 2019, Ryuho Okawa held a lecture entitled, "Hope for the Future," at the Hiroshima Prefectural Culture and Arts Hall.

and Nagasaki was because they saw the Japanese people as "yellow monkeys." This was why it didn't matter to them how many people they killed. In their minds, Japanese people weren't human beings and didn't possess souls. I don't think they could have committed such actions unless they had convinced themselves of that.

So, I think that what came out of my marriage to Yoko Ono would have been different had I married an American or a British. At that time, the American leaders who had fought World War II probably wanted Japan to be seen as the Devil's country still.

So, in other words, they probably thought of me as a delinquent. Since I had been to India, I could understand, in a way, why the Japanese fought a war for racial liberation.

India might have appeared to be a country behind the times, but it is also a country with a long history and tradition, and its independence from the long British occupation was thanks to the strong blow the British received from the Japanese. I was also affected by Gandhi, too. There were things like that, and I don't think I was fully understood. People probably thought I was strange or eccentric.

At the least, I was able to send out the message that a large war is not desirable and that racial discrimination policies are wrong. I feel that our huge concerts in the United States, which got broadcasted throughout the world, also led to the racial discrimination policies being abolished. This became one of the jobs that I accomplished.

TAKEUCHI

When you visited the Yasukuni Shrine, back then, was that a thought that you had in mind?

JOHN LENNON

Well I often visited Japan. I came here many times. I wanted to study the Japanese culture and I think that the Americans who destroyed Japan didn't know much about the Japanese culture, so if they had known more about it, I think that they would have given more thought to what they were doing.

In the back of my mind, I always had the sense that I was an alien, or a stranger. I didn't know where that came from, but I had the feeling that something was wrong about believing in the white dominance theory.

NAKATA
You probably gave the Western people an opportunity to notice the great aspects of Japan. We are thankful to your marriage to Yoko Ono and for often visiting Karuizawa, because we think that that must have also had an influence.

JOHN LENNON
Hahaha [*laughs*]. Yeah.

5

On His Love, His Song "Imagine," and Jesus Christ

Reflections on His Family

NAKATA

When you were active as a Beatles member, you gave many messages of love.

JOHN LENNON

Yeah, yeah, yeah, yeah, yeah.

NAKATA

For example, you sang "All You Need Is Love" for a live TV broadcast that aired worldwide. And after you married Yoko Ono, you gave many messages of love and messages against war. Did your way of thinking about love change after getting married to Yoko?

JOHN LENNON

Hmmm... Well, how I think about love is hard to define. I think it also gradually changes with your age. Hmmm, well... There were childlike aspects to myself, and it was hard for me to think in terms of the legal-rights perspective. Yoko had a child in her previous marriage, and once, we brought her daughter to our hotel to play with her, but then, we were accused of kidnapping and confining her [*smiles wryly*]. I have a slight tendency for laxness regarding things like that. Also, we went through three miscarriages and faced some tough times. I don't fully know about what it is like to grow a happy and healthy family; I only understand about raising a child to the age of five. I'm a little bit like a boxer, in this meaning. The majority of boxers come to the end of their careers when they are around age thirty, so I was maybe similar to that.

Well...what is love? I really don't know much about that, but it was very tough creating family love. I just still felt lonely by myself to the point of unbearable feelings, that I needed to call over Yoko. When we had our child, I was very happy about that. He's still alive, but having been born to a parent like me, I can imagine the heavy burden they've had to bear and how difficult it must have been for them. I couldn't fully fulfill my role as their father, so, hmm, I feel I just left them the heavy burden of the "legend" to bear.

He reached many people with his messages

JOHN LENNON

There also were quite a few criticisms about my wife, and there were times when my relationship with the other Beatles members was not going well. Well, I think it is different with men and women, but I experienced that liking someone could mean your other human relationships could become broken. I was not getting along with the other members of the Beatles, and I think that had something to do with the disbanding of the Beatles.

Well...but I'd like to accept all of it as destiny. I want to accept all of it as destiny. I think, on Earth, it is better to experience love for the opposite sex and parental love, but I could not fulfill them completely. I also think that in the later years of my life, I continued singing songs of encouragement for the sake of society, the weak, the underprivileged, and those without power.

But still, it is really hard to fight against weaponed people. After all, there were things that I couldn't protect as an individual. It seems when Mr. Ryuho Okawa went to see the Dakota House, he could see how I could get assassinated by living there. The small path beside the building was crime-filled, and you'd park your car on the curb and then take the steps leading up to the front door, so I was in clear sight of others when going in and out of my home. Someone could be easily assassinated in a place like that, especially considering that 40-something percent of Americans owned guns.

It must have been very easy to assassinate me. That was something about me. So, maybe I should have searched for a place where I wouldn't be easily assassinated. I guess I could have lived around Liverpool. Well, that's the kind of person I was, so it can't be helped. That's the kind of thing that I don't realize about. So, it can't be helped.

Well...what is love?... I don't know. But I feel I gave a lot to many people. Not that I remember the faces of everyone, but I reached many people with my feelings and messages to the fullest that I could convey them. I am very happy our songs are still being played. Yeah, that's how I feel.

His true message in "Imagine"

TAKEUCHI

What was the love you put into "Imagine"?

JOHN LENNON

Hmmm, people misunderstood the meaning that I gave "Imagine." This happened during the Nixon and Johnson eras, a time of the bombings of North Vietnam. What I was singing in this song was that our imagination has the power to create the future. And so, I was singing about the power of our mind, but politically, they did not see it that way. They thought I was clearly directing the anti-war movement and inspiring everyone from behind, and that if everyone on the battlefield heard such a poisonous song, then everyone would lose the will to fight. This is how they took this song to be. Well, I guess it was seen at that time as a culture corrupting America.

I was saying an ideal future can be created through the power of the mind, which is a religious meaning, a teaching religious leaders would be preaching on. But people in the real world did not realize this meaning and thought I was commanding a clear anti-war campaign.

The real being who said, "We're more popular than Jesus now."

TAKEUCHI
Another misunderstood case is your remark about Jesus Christ.*

JOHN LENNON
Oh, yes, that too.

TAKEUCHI
When you said, "We're more popular than Jesus

---

* See p.47 in chapter one.

now," news of this was heard around the world, but some people said that it could be an antithesis to the church disciples who are twisting the teachings. I myself feel that the true meaning of this comment about Christ was a message to the Vatican or the Church of England. Could you tell us what you were really saying through this remark about Jesus?

JOHN LENNON

Some people might not know about what happened. I said, "Christianity will go," and, "We're more popular than Jesus now," on some occasion.

And I had to give an apology later on. I made the excuse that I shouldn't have referred to ourselves, and that I should have said that the television became more influential than Jesus. But what I said was actually my true feelings.

TAKEUCHI

I see.

JOHN LENNON

Well, although I didn't realize when I was alive that my soul was connected to Jesus, those words were Jesus' real feelings flowing through me.

TAKEUCHI

Ah, yes.

JOHN LENNON

In Jesus' eyes, the church was corrupted to the core. It was over, in his view, and this was what Jesus basically wanted to say, and his feelings became mixed into my words.

TAKEUCHI

Ah, I see...

JOHN LENNON

My words included them. They got into my channel, and I spoke them. So, "Christianity will go," were actually the words of Jesus.

As Jesus, I said, "Christianity will go," but the church retaliated against it, as if to say, "If that's the case, then we will kill Jesus." It's exactly as Dostoevsky said. It's the grand inquisitor in *The Karamazov Brothers*. He wrote about Jesus, who was reborn in the sixteenth century or so and healed the sick. Knowing that this person was Jesus reborn, the grand inquisitor captured him anyway.

And he says to Jesus, "We know who you are. Why did you come now? We don't need you. We have taken over the church." "We" is the Devil. So, he was saying that the Devil has taken over the church, and that Jesus isn't needed there, and doesn't need to come now. The grand inquisitor didn't kill him, but he took him out of the town and exiled him, telling him never to return and appear there again.

This was Dostoevsky's own inspiration that told him if Jesus returned now, he would also be persecuted by the church as Jan Hus and Joan of Arc had been. And this would actually occur in reality in later years.

He just knew that something was wrong about the Christian Church

JOHN LENNON

So, hmmm, I didn't want to say that I was greater than Christ. But if Jesus could see the Christian Church, the churches around the world, such as the American churches, the Church of England, and the Vatican Church, my intuition told me that he would have said, "This is not what I told them to do."

TAKEUCHI

I see.

JOHN LENNON

And that slipped through my lips. I always had a habit of speaking straightforwardly, and I didn't study about being careful of that. I hadn't trained myself to speak bureaucratically and cautiously, and so I couldn't talk in that kind of way. Also, I had feelings strongly disagreeing with the bureaucratic, tax-office-like tendencies of the church. It didn't feel to be the essence of Jesus. And I wanted to say the church has become the Jews of Jesus' time who persecuted him, that it is the Christian Church who've become them.

We became a very big name, and when I returned the MBE medal to the Queen, maybe they started to see me as some kind of anti-nationalist. Towards the end, my wife and I had even imagined the mad idea of creating a country of our own, haha [*laughs*].

I just knew that something was wrong, and this feeling kept coming to me over and over in my heart, but I thought, "How come? I don't know why. Maybe because I'm rock?" But it must have been Jesus's own feelings I was feeling.

So, this means, when Jesus' feelings began to express through me, I was persecuted and killed as Jesus had been.

His feelings regarding the Vietnam War

TAKEUCHI

The lyrics to "Imagine" say, "There's no heaven," and, "No hell below us." Were they including criticisms about medieval Christianity that pressured monarchies in various ways? Did each of your songs, in truth, contain Jesus' feelings about the current church system?

JOHN LENNON

In the past, there were many religions that suffered oppression by Christianity and there were also invasions into other countries. I knew about that. But it was already an ancient part of history and talking about that wouldn't have helped anything.

But something like it happened recently. We saw World War II happen in front of our eyes, and American imperialism afterwards bullied the weak. This is what the Vietnam War basically was... Though, since my albums weren't selling in communist countries, I didn't have any intention to support the communists either.

North Vietnam fought against South Vietnam, and although the younger people probably don't know this, the Americans supported South Vietnam and fought a guerrilla war with the North. But, in reality, the North had the Chinese army supplying them with goods and even fighter aircraft.

They (the Americans) developed Napalm, which is a kind of firebomb that burned the surroundings very well and there was also Agent Orange, a defoliant. In other words, the trees hid the guerrilla soldiers, so they forced the leaves to fall off to expose the guerrilla soldiers, and then they burned the soldiers with napalm. So, what they were burning were actually thatched-roof farmhouses. And when I saw people being burned and killed, I felt that this was not something a human being would do. I never witnessed an actual witch-hunting in the Middle Ages, but it was not something a human being or any truly Christian country would do. But at the same time, I never thought that communism was right, either. If you give power to the people, they will think about what is truly important to them, and they will try to protect that.

There is indeed what is called the domino theory that says that communism could spread and this needs to be prevented. But Saigon fell, in the end. On the television, they showed the Americans escaping on helicopters.

Then, the communists also took over South Vietnam. In the end, Vietnam's national circumstances have changed now. They are wary of China and seeking the aid of the United States and Japan.

So, you shouldn't look at the short-term, and instead, people need to decide for themselves. Communism, with its single-person dictatorship, can be very scary, it's true. But non-communist countries are also scary when they possess enough immense power to invade and destroy other countries. If I could have lived longer, I might have also sung anti-war songs about the Gulf War and the Iraq War. So, my death probably benefited America, I'm pretty sure of that [*laughs*].

6

His Message to Everyone

His message to Yoko Ono and Paul McCartney

TAKEUCHI

Ms. Yoko Ono and Mr. Paul McCartney are both still alive in this world, so if you could leave your messages for them here.

JOHN LENNON

I think Paul has been doing the best he can for a long time. He is two years younger than me. He is still very active and came to Japan and performed at Tokyo Dome at the age of seventy-something. He's incredible. Really, my hats off to him. He really has stuck to it. As long as there is even just one person like him, our songs can continue to be sung. And he has written many songs, afterward, too, and received many awards.

So everything has gone well with him, hasn't it? He's really succeeded as a musician.

And then...I think Yoko, how do I say this, really, she continued to always be my support for my political ideas. Many people said that my political side was a little crazy, but it is an issue where there continues to be a need for it. This is the reason they didn't want people to play "Imagine" after the passenger planes crashed into the World Trade Center. It sounds as if it's telling people to "imagine world peace." And they didn't want people to feel that. They wanted people's fighting spirit instead. The United States went on to "destroy" Iraq as a country, very quickly too. It was as if to say, "We hope this will show you what will happen when the United States really gets angry." It's as if they were a huge gorilla, a "King Kong," saying, "We will crush your country if you destroy two buildings of ours." That is the kind of fighting that they showed.

Well, I can understand the anger. I understand the anger, but thousands of Americans died, and hundreds of thousands of Iraqis also died, and the war is still ongoing, isn't it? While changing its form, it has continued and spread to Syria and Turkey, hasn't it? The chain of hatred does not end, and it will not end forever. So, it has to be stopped somewhere.

I think Japan is great in that aspect. The Japanese were inflicted with much damage in the war, but the Japanese became friends with the United States and tried to revive itself into international society, didn't they? I think that is a fine thing to have done. So, we need to have that kind of feeling and cut the chain of hatred. Most Muslims also cannot cut the chain of hatred. I don't think their religious founder gave them such a teaching to begin with. Even God hasn't taught them this, so they need to get past that somewhere.

If they cannot overcome this, then by singing the same song, people of different religions can gather under that song. This is what I was "imagining."

"Ryuho Okawa and I are doing the same things"

TAKEUCHI

I think when you passed away, the whole world was engulfed in sadness. So last but not least, could you give us a message for your fans around the world?

JOHN LENNON

John Lennon still lives. And I am about to bring my soul to Happy Science. Through Happy Science, I will be able to express my spirit of love and peace as well as my spirit as an artist.

There might be some slight differences regarding the methods and the way of thinking that Mr. Ryuho Okawa and I have, but what we are doing is the same. So, if "Imagine" and "Power to the People" were to be played in China, the tyranny of China would collapse. But I think that they will still refuse to play them there.

Aren't the teachings of Happy Science also trying to destroy such things? And also in North Korea? So, even if the methods are different, we are, in truth, doing the same things. And Mr. Ryuho Okawa is calling for national defense, so that may sound like he is a militarist, but I don't think he is telling you that you ought to actively invade other countries and enslave them. He is saying that you shouldn't become a defenseless country open to invasion. I think he is telling you to take caution and try to prevent that in advance. The fact is that both our aims are to promote peace. Master Okawa is saying peace should be built upon justice, because he is pursuing world justice.

This is the reason he is voicing opinions against the frightful China, the country of 1.4 billion people, and Mr. Abe is hard at work trying to bring together a Japan-Russia Peace Treaty by going to Russia, even though he's had a tough time. The reason he is doing this is because he understands Mr. Ryuho Okawa's strategy of containing China. Progress won't be made only by giving priority to territory. And he realizes that as the United States gradually weakens, it's possible Japan won't stand a chance against China and Russia if they joined forces, and so he understands that he needs Russia on his side. Of course, the mass media isn't reporting this in this way, but he is well aware of that. So he is carrying out a way to change China's imperialism and hegemonism into a democracy.

So, that is why you are trying different approaches, isn't it? You're giving teachings, creating movies, producing music, and doing various activities. But what we are thinking about is the same.

You were playing a little bit of the song "Power to the People" when I came here, but if that song starts to get played in Beijing, then Xi Jinping's regime will be close to the end. There is no mistaking it. Even without it, if your movie, *The Laws of the Universe-Part I*, was shown in Beijing, then the destruction of that regime will be near. Ryuho Okawa and I are doing the same things, in the end.

A war of values is going on in the world of arts

JOHN LENNON

Yesterday, you couldn't win the Academy Award and probably were upset and couldn't sleep, right?

TAKEUCHI

Yes. I was really regretful. Yes.

JOHN LENNON

Well, that's okay because you are ready with "Part II" and "Part III." All you need is to keep on firing continuous bullets. You shouldn't think that everything's over already, because you're not an organization that gains power from being recognized by already existing things. You are creating a brand of your own. You just need to keep continuing the "Ryuho Okawa brand." You're supposed to be giving out "Ryuho Okawa Awards" because, honestly, you're superior to the Academy Awards.

Well, I returned the highest medal I could get from the U.K., but I feel Mr. Ryuho Okawa will not accept the National Honor Award from the Prime Minister even if he says he will bestow it on him. That is how it is, because we have been the ones leading. It's only natural. It's better to have this kind of a spirit in yourselves.

Your works have a very deep-thinking nature. You are competing in the entertainment world of animation where there are competitors winning box-office revenue for their entertaining value. You're trying to win against them with works with deep-thinking nature. They're difficult for children to understand, and it can be tough for people to accept them easily. So, you shouldn't concern yourself about this and find your own way. Some aspects will be accepted and some won't.

You see, a war of values is now going on in the world of the arts. You can clearly see that hero-themed movies aren't receiving the Academy Awards. The Avengers-based movies haven't received them, have they? It's been the same situation with you. Movies depicting evil worlds or people who get possessed by criminal minds and drive themselves into that world get awarded more easily, even when they are live-action movies.

So well, it's best not to give much trust to the things of this world. I think that the same goes with the Academy Awards in Japan. Criminal-themed and murder-themed movies receive awards much more easily, don't they? But you wouldn't be able to create movies like that. You definitely wouldn't be able to create a movie like *Shoplifters*. You see?

TAKEUCHI
We wouldn't. Yes.

JOHN LENNON
You definitely couldn't make a movie like *Shoplifters*. If we look at the reason that it won an award, it received an award in France first, and the movie's content is a modern, compact version of Victor Hugo's *Les Miserables* trying to justify that kind of theme. It's portraying a value perspective that blames society for people becoming shoplifters, and tries to say how heart-warming it is that strangers can live in harmony together.

TAKEUCHI
Yes.

JOHN LENNON

But this is not a value that ought to be spread around the world. And if it receives an Academy Award in the United States, then it will create havoc not only in Japan, but everywhere else, also. Everyone will start to think that it's okay to do such a thing, and will start to copy it.

So, prizes should be awarded to good values, but the leftist values want the opposite values to receive more notice. I think we should be cautious about this kind of thing. There are many things that I feel we should be cautious about.

And so many of them are about murder mysteries, aren't they? Hmm.

"Can you tell the difference between Queen and the Beatles?"

JOHN LENNON

In the best picture category for live-action movies for the Academy Awards, I think that *Bohemian*

Rhapsody is in the lead, right now. Although we are both British bands, people can't tell the difference between Queen and the Beatles. Even rock fans really can't recognize much of a difference. I guess people are moved by Queen, but as you have learned already in your research, the soul of the leader of Queen is lost.* He thought he committed good acts, but his soul is lost. On the other hand, I, who was assassinated, seem to have returned to a high world in Heaven, and though I said that I surpassed Jesus and someone killed me, I've been "resurrected" and am saying things. It might make them want to shoot another bullet at me in the other world, I really think so.

Can you tell the difference between Queen and the Beatles? Is that difficult to do? Even rock has differences. Many movies were made about us, but our inner spiritual aspect wasn't depicted

---

* See the spiritual message held on January, 12, 2019, entitled, "Spiritual Messages from Freddie Mercury and Zoroaster."

in some of them, and they portrayed us instead as delinquents. It's sad to say so.

If you just look at our exterior, we may seem that way, it's true, but we had something noble within ourselves. We had something universal. It's whether you can sense this or not.

So we aren't leftists, and we aren't saying that people should completely abandon self-effort. We aren't saying all evil in society is the responsibility of the government or people with power. Well, I think that Master Okawa will help amend that misconception.

You have said that Dickens, the author of *Christmas Carol*, has not gone to Heaven.[*] But that was the time of Britain's Labor Party and the era where social evil originated from. It developed out of the idea that the wealthy are taking all the wealth and causing poverty in others, so their

---

[*] See Sayaka Okawa, *Okawa Sayaka No Bungaku No Susume: Sekaibungaku-hen, Jo* [Sayaka Okawa's Introduction to Literature: World Literature, Volume 1] (Tokyo: IRH Press, 2016). Available in the Japanese edition only.

wealth should be distributed to others. You can't tell just by reading his novels themselves, but that is what he was trying to say, in the end, wasn't it? But this idea, in the end, leads all the way to the Devil's teachings.

"Globalism without a savior is destruction"

JOHN LENNON

There are things I want to also say about the EU, now. There are similar issues. Even though communism fell, it seems they are trying to create another group of communist countries again. And the U.K. is suffering now. They want to regain sovereignty, but they don't want to be completely isolated, either. Isn't that what they're troubled by? Mr. Trump is very bold, isn't he? He is absolutely bold.

If I were still alive, then there is about a 50 percent possibility that I would be singing an opposition song against Trump. But his way of thinking says that people need to rebuild their country by themselves, doesn't it? Yeah. So, I think that's fine, too. Globalism is nearing its end; this is what is happening. Globalism without a savior is destruction, in the end. This is what's being proved, now.

Japan is a country that is right in the middle of this course and is suffering. Japan believes globalism is ending, but also feels it's safer to stay on the globalism bandwagon. So, Japan is sending friendly glances at the EU, China, and the United States. But meanwhile, Japan is not sure what it should do. So, I think that Carlos Ghosn's arrest at Nissan* and the refusal to release him are signaling the end of globalism. That's my sense. I think this is Japan's display of

---

* On November 19, 2018, Nissan's Former Chairman and CEO Carlos Ghosn was charged for misreporting his remuneration in securities reports and arrested for financial misconduct. He was also indicted on breach of trust. His detainment lasted two months. After release on bail, he fled to Lebanon. His arrest is now an international issue involving the Japanese and French governments.

their determination to stop foreign capital from controlling their country. Because the Japanese government is aware of what it is doing.

This is illegal, what they are doing. To refuse to release someone with that much social standing is unthinkable, because he isn't a natural criminal and he didn't commit murder or theft. But this is Japan's way of trying to cut ties with globalism. So they are letting it be known that they won't allow foreign companies to control Japanese companies. By showing that they will go that far, foreign companies in Japan will lose their desire to buy up Japanese companies, won't they? Yeah. People wouldn't want to ever take up residence in Japan, don't you think? That is their aim. It is a political message. So this was a display of their intention to let Japanese companies sweep the world once more, but not let foreign capital dominate Japanese companies. Well it is kind of like pitching the strength of one country against the other, France vs. Japan. That is how we have to look at it.

So now, we are witnessing the political clash between globalism and state sovereignty. There is righteous nationalism that was started by Mr. Trump that says a nation's people need to take care of their country by themselves, rebuild it, and nourish their own people. And opposite that there is globalism that says everyone can join hands.

This is very complicated, so I can't explain this any further. From here on is the job for El Cantare. So, I cannot speak further on this. All I can create are songs. I can't say any more on this, but apparently, this is that kind of era. So instead of giving "power to the people," we need to start giving "power to El Cantare" from now on. We need to further spread El Cantare's thinking. This means that "we love El Cantare," and in addition to that, "Jesus loves El Cantare." We need to hand everything over to El Cantare now, because unless we do, we cannot successfully manage the Earth. I really think so.

People like myself and the space being calling himself Paul McCartney have come to you, and we are giving you our support because we want you to know that such an age has come, now. In other words, there are many beings who are cheering you on.

In time, there will be "a landslide"

JOHN LENNON
But just yesterday, the space beings were also disappointed about the Academy Award that you didn't win.*

TAKEUCHI
Oh, really [*smiles wryly*]?

---

* For the movie, *The Laws of the Universe-Part I.*

JOHN LENNON

Yes. They were saying, "Our time has been delayed a bit. If only this movie would spread a little more. If *The Laws of the Universe* gained a bit more recognition and global acceptance, then we would be able to contact Earth a bit sooner. This has slowed us down one step. Let's look forward to three years from now."

They don't visibly show themselves, so people don't realize whether they exist or not. What a pity... From the perspective of the space beings, it's movies without value that are winning awards. It's been very disappointing to them. So, I am indirectly telling you what they said. Yeah. Because I have sometimes spoken with them.

TAKEUCHI

I see.

JOHN LENNON

Yeah, yeah. Indirectly. Since the space beings and the Beatles are all cheering for you, "something" will eventually happen like a landslide. You can be sure of that. But you need to store up your strength to be ready for that, yeah.

TAKEUCHI

Yes. Thank you very much. We learned, today, that you are in Heaven, and continuing even now to love the people of the world. We also heard your various thoughts on the political, religious, and global conditions of today. Thank you very much.

JOHN LENNON

Yes, you all need to study up on *Kuro-Obi Eigo* (lit. Black Belt in English).

TAKEUCHI

Oh, yes.

JOHN LENNON

The reason you didn't win might be because your speech in the United States didn't have effect.

TAKEUCHI

[*Smiles wryly*] I see. That might be true. I am very sorry.

JOHN LENNON

If your English were more powerful and electric, you almost might have won. It's possible.

TAKEUCHI

I will do my very best.

JOHN LENNON

I mean, I don't want to threaten you too much. But for now, don't give up too easily.

TAKEUCHI

Yes.

JOHN LENNON

Sometimes, success can explode once, but these are mainly short-lived, so if you really want to succeed, it is better to create one wave after another wave, like water gradually surging in. I think this is important. Well, I am looking forward to your success, and will continue to support you.

TAKEUCHI

Thank you very much. We'll try our best.

JOHN LENNON

Yeah, let's try the best you can.

TAKEUCHI

Yes. We'll try our best.

The more you age,
the more your voice has influence

JOHN LENNON
[*Speaking to Nakata*] Was there more that you wanted to ask me?

NAKATA
Thank you very much. I'm alright.

JOHN LENNON
I guess we are finished then. You know, I can't tell what his age is [*referring to Nakata*]. Are you younger than me?

NAKATA
I'm sixty-four.

JOHN LENNON
Really? You're that young? I'm sorry about that.

NAKATA
[*Laughs*].

JOHN LENNON
Well, there is a bit more of the youthful spirit in me. Well, it's a good thing for you, because the more you age, the more your voice has influence. When everyone is young, other people may think you are a little crazy, so it's important to be careful about that. And what you say receives more trust when you are someone of a certain age, cultivation, and experience. This is an important thing.

TAKEUCHI
Yes.

JOHN LENNON
Well, let's do your best, one stage higher. Since the start of the new year, Master Okawa has been also diligently working little by little on something.

He has been working little by little by little by little on things that make us who are watching wonder to ourselves, "What could he be doing this for?" And when he was upstairs, today, he spent two or three minutes debating very busily and seriously whether or not he should wear the round glasses that his secretary had prepared.

TAKEUCHI
Oh, I see [*laughs*].

JOHN LENNON
In the end, they concluded not to, because he's not doing an impersonation of me. The Aide to Master and CEO made this decision as her job, and he appeared today without the glasses. So, there are rather many "difficult jobs" in this world.

TAKEUCHI
Yes [*laughs*].

JOHN LENNON

Well, I'll stop talking about things happening backstage, and for the time being, we are putting a lot of hopes on you, so please try your best to make progress.

TAKEUCHI

Thank you very much for today.

JOHN LENNON

Yes.

7

Concluding Comments Regarding John Lennon's Astonishing Spiritual Message

The insert song to *The Laws of the Universe-Part 0* suddenly came from John Lennon

RYUHO OKAWA

[*Claps his hands three times*] We've now held three spiritual messages from John Lennon already.

But nevertheless, I was astonished to find out John Lennon was a branch spirit or brother soul of Jesus Christ. In the movie, *The Laws of the Universe-Part 0*, we included a song in English called "Lost Love," and it came from John Lennon, actually. John Lennon's spirit suddenly visited me, created this song, and left. But I had no idea at all why he visited me. As a youth, I wasn't a die-hard fan of the Beatles, so I couldn't find the reason he would visit me suddenly. So,

I thought of holding a spiritual message by him, but since music is difficult to discuss in words, we put that aside.

Since then, the entertainment division of Happy Science gradually progressed and Jesus also came to me and started to create songs for us. Several of our songs were created in this way.

It felt kind of strange to me, and now, the dots are finally starting to connect.

For example, Happy Science Academy's pep song (called, "*Erabareshi Monotachi Yo* [My Chosen People]"), was actually created through Jesus Christ's assistance. Jesus Christ composed those lyrics, and so they might amaze you.

The songs in Happy Science movies have value

RYUHO OKAWA

And recently, Jesus Christ assisted me when I composed the song and lyrics to the main theme song of Happy Science's documentary movie called *Heart to Heart** and *Life Is Beautiful*†.

So, I wondered, "Why is this?" And now I understand that John Lennon was behind it, and this means that those songs have value.

TAKEUCHI

Yes.

RYUHO OKAWA

Heart to Heart will be shown in only two theatres, and I said, "What a waste," but there was one stubborn (disciple) of mine who insisted on showing it in one theatre in Tokyo, and another one in Osaka. I thought that since Jesus created the song for this movie, it would be better if many people could have the chance to hear it. But it seems that things in this world don't work

---

* Released in 2018, this film's original concept was authored by Ryuho Okawa.

† Released in 2019, this film's original concept was authored by Ryuho Okawa.

out smoothly all the time. I think that we didn't have confidence in this movie. Next time, they are going to expand the number of theaters our movies will be shown at. We have been receiving a lot of guidance like this from Heaven, so we need to have more confidence. We must strive to become people of that capacity.

TAKEUCHI

Yes, we will try harder. Thank you very much.

Afterword

It is as if the world of music is closing in on me.

A bookworm since my early days, I rather disliked rock since it made it hard for me to focus on my reading.

But in order to change the world, I need the spirit of rock in my actions. I began to think so.

We lived in the same age and with the same aspiration, but it is difficult to understand each other.

Now, inspirations for songs come down to me one after another from John Lennon who is in Heaven, but I do not think we are accepting them enough, and I feel they are going to waste.

However, the messages for Happy Science are clear: "Change the world." "Don't stay as just one of the religions in Japan."

I must think harder and harder and invent "uncle rock." Life is surprisingly tough, and our workbook of problems continues.

Ryuho Okawa
Master & CEO of Happy Science Group
February 1, 2019

ABOUT THE AUTHOR

RYUHO OKAWA was born on July 7th 1956, in Tokushima prefecture, Japan. After graduating from the University of Tokyo with a law degree, he joined a Tokyo-based trading house. While working at its New York headquarters, he studied international finance at the Graduate Center of the City University of New York. In 1981, he attained Great Enlightenment and became aware that he is El Cantare with a mission to bring salvation to all of humankind. In 1986 he established Happy Science. It now has members in over 100 countries across the world, with more than 700 local branches and temples as well as 10,000 missionary houses around the world. The total number of lectures has exceeded 3,100 (of which more than 150 are in English) and over 2,600 books (of which more than 500 are Spiritual Interview Series) have been published, many of which are translated into 31 languages. Many of the books, including *The Laws of the Sun* have become best sellers or million sellers. To date, Happy Science has produced 20 movies. The original story and original concept were given by the Executive Producer Ryuho Okawa. Recent movie titles are *The Real Exorcist* (live-action movie to be released in May 2020), *Kiseki to no Deai - Kokoro ni Yorisou 3 -* (lit. "Encounters with Miracles - Heart to Heart 3 -," documentary scheduled to be released in Aug. 2020), and *Twiceborn* (live-action movie to be released in Fall of 2020). He has also composed the lyrics and music of over 100 songs, such as theme songs and featured songs of movies. Moreover, he is the Founder of Happy Science University and Happy Science Academy (Junior and Senior High School), Founder and President of the Happiness Realization Party, Founder and Honorary Headmaster of Happy Science Institute of Government and Management, Founder of IRH Press Co., Ltd., and the Chairperson of New Star Production Co., Ltd. and ARI Production Co., Ltd.

WHAT IS EL CANTARE?

El Cantare means "the Light of the Earth," and is the Supreme God of the Earth who has been guiding humankind since the beginning of Genesis. He is whom Jesus called Father and Muhammad called Allah. Different parts of El Cantare's core consciousness have descended to Earth in the past, once as Alpha and another as Elohim. His branch spirits, such as Shakyamuni Buddha and Hermes, have descended to Earth many times and helped to flourish many civilizations. To unite various religions and to integrate various fields of study in order to build a new civilization on Earth, a part of the core consciousness has descended to Earth as Master Ryuho Okawa.

El Cantare, God of the Earth

Ra Mu
17,000 years ago

Alpha
330 million years ago

Elohim
150 million years ago

Shakyamuni Buddha
2,600 years ago

Thoth
12,000 years ago

Hermes
4,300 years ago

Rient Arl Croud
7,000 years ago

Ophealis
6,500 years ago

Ryuho Okawa

Alpha Alpha is a part of the core consciousness of El Cantare that descended to Earth more than 300 million years ago. Alpha preached Earth's Truths to harmonize and unify Earth-born humans and space people who came from other planets.

Elohim Elohim is the name of El Cantare's core consciousness that lived on Earth 150 million years ago. He taught teachings of wisdom, mainly on the differences of light and darkness, good and evil.

Shakyamuni Buddha Gautama Siddhartha was born as a prince into the Shakya Clan in India around 2,600 years ago. When he was 29 years old, he renounced the world and sought enlightenment. He later attained Great Enlightenment and founded Buddhism.

Hermes In the Greek mythology, Hermes is thought of as one of the 12 Olympian gods, but the spiritual Truth is that he taught the teachings of love and progress around 4,300 years ago that became the origin of the current Western civilization. He is a hero that truly existed.

Ophealis Ophealis was born in Greece around 6,500 years ago and was the leader who took an expedition to as far as Egypt. He is the God of miracles, prosperity, and arts, and is known as Osiris in the Egyptian mythology.

Rient Arl Croud Rient Arl Croud was born as a king of the ancient Incan Empire around 7,000 years ago and taught about the mysteries of the mind. In the heavenly world, he is responsible for the interactions that take place between various planets.

Thoth Thoth was an almighty leader who built the golden age of the Atlantic civilization around 12,000 years ago. In the Egyptian mythology, he is known as God Thoth.

Ra Mu Ra Mu was a leader who built the golden age of the civilization of Mu around 17,000 years ago. As a religious leader and a politician, he ruled by uniting religion and politics.

WHAT IS A SPIRITUAL MESSAGE?

We are all spiritual beings living on this earth. The following is the mechanism behind Master Ryuho Okawa's spiritual messages.

1 You are a spirit

People are born into this world to gain wisdom through various experiences and return to the other world when their lives end. We are all spirits and repeat this cycle in order to refine our souls.

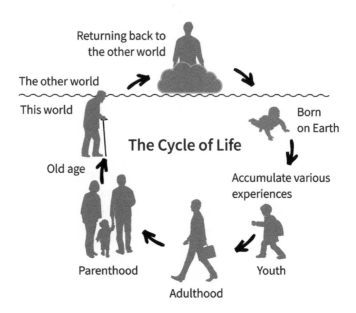

2 You have a guardian spirit

Guardian spirits are those who protect the people who are living on this earth. Each of us has a guardian spirit that watches over us and guides us from the other world. They were us in our past life, and are identical in how we think.

3 How spiritual messages work

Master Ryuho Okawa, through his enlightenment, is capable of summoning any spirit from anywhere in the world, including the spirit world.

Master Okawa's way of receiving spiritual messages is fundamentally different from that of other psychic mediums who undergo trances and are thereby completely taken over by the spirits they are channeling.

Master Okawa's attainment of a high level of enlightenment enables him to retain full control of his consciousness and body throughout the duration of the spiritual message. To allow the spirits to express their own thoughts and personalities freely, however, Master Okawa usually softens the dominancy of his consciousness. This way, he is able to keep his own philosophies out of the way and ensure that the spiritual messages are pure expressions of the spirits he is channeling.

Since guardian spirits think at the same subconscious level as the person living on earth, Master Okawa can summon the spirit and find out what the person on earth is actually thinking. If the person has already returned to the other world, the spirit can give messages to the people living on earth through Master Okawa.

Since 2009, more than 1,000 sessions of spiritual messages have been openly recorded by Master Okawa, and the majority of these have been published. Spiritual messages from the guardian spirits of people living today such as U.S. President Donald Trump, Japanese Prime Minister Shinzo Abe and Chinese President Xi Jinping, as well as spiritual messages sent from the spirit world by Jesus Christ, Muhammad, Thomas Edison, Mother Teresa, Steve Jobs and Nelson Mandela are just a tiny pack of spiritual messages that were published so far.

Domestically, in Japan, these spiritual messages are being read by a wide range of politicians and mass media, and the high-level contents of these books are delivering an impact even more on politics, news and public opinion. In recent years, there have been spiritual messages recorded in English, and English translations are being done on the spiritual messages given in Japanese. These have been published overseas, one after another, and have started to shake the world.

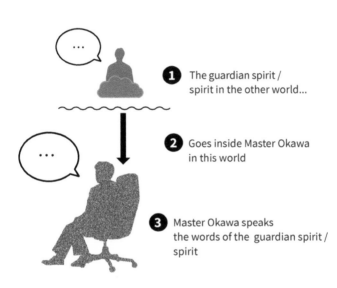

1 The guardian spirit / spirit in the other world...

2 Goes inside Master Okawa in this world

3 Master Okawa speaks the words of the guardian spirit / spirit

*For more about spiritual messages and a complete list of books in the Spiritual Interview Series, visit **okawabooks.com***

ABOUT HAPPY SCIENCE

Happy Science is a global movement that empowers individuals to find purpose and spiritual happiness and to share that happiness with their families, societies, and the world. With more than twelve million members around the world, Happy Science aims to increase awareness of spiritual truths and expand our capacity for love, compassion, and joy so that together we can create the kind of world we all wish to live in.

Activities at Happy Science are based on the Principles of Happiness (Love, Wisdom, Self-Reflection, and Progress). These principles embrace worldwide philosophies and beliefs, transcending boundaries of culture and religions.

Love teaches us to give ourselves freely without expecting anything in return; it encompasses giving, nurturing, and forgiving.

Wisdom leads us to the insights of spiritual truths, and opens us to the true meaning of life and the will of God (the universe, the highest power, Buddha).

Self-Reflection brings a mindful, nonjudgmental lens to our thoughts and actions to help us find our truest selves—the essence of our souls—and deepen our connection to the highest power. It helps us attain a clean and peaceful mind and leads us to the right life path.

Progress emphasizes the positive, dynamic aspects of our spiritual growth—actions we can take to manifest and spread happiness around the world. It's a path that not only expands our soul growth, but also furthers the collective potential of the world we live in.

PROGRAMS AND EVENTS

The doors of Happy Science are open to all. We offer a variety of programs and events, including self-exploration and self-growth programs, spiritual seminars, meditation and contemplation sessions, study groups, and book events.

Our programs are designed to:
* Deepen your understanding of your purpose and meaning in life
* Improve your relationships and increase your capacity to love unconditionally
* Attain peace of mind, decrease anxiety and stress, and feel positive
* Gain deeper insights and a broader perspective on the world
* Learn how to overcome life's challenges
  ... and much more.

*For more information, visit **happy-science.org**.*

OUR ACTIVITIES

Happy Science does other various activities to provide support for those in need.

◆ **You Are An Angel! General Incorporated Association**

Happy Science has a volunteer network in Japan that encourages and supports children with disabilities as well as their parents and guardians.

◆ **Never Mind School for Truancy**

At 'Never Mind,' we support students who find it very challenging to attend schools in Japan. We also nurture their self-help spirit and power to rebound against obstacles in life based on Master Okawa's teachings and faith.

◆ **"Prevention Against Suicide" Campaign since 2003**

A nationwide campaign to reduce suicides; over 20,000 people commit suicide every year in Japan. "The Suicide Prevention Website-Words of Truth for You-" presents spiritual prescriptions for worries such as depression, lost love, extramarital affairs, bullying and work-related problems, thereby saving many lives.

◆ **Support for Anti-bullying Campaigns**

Happy Science provides support for a group of parents and guardians, Network to Protect Children from Bullying, a general incorporated foundation launched in Japan to end bullying, including those that can even be called a criminal offense. So far, the network received more than 5,000 cases and resolved 90% of them.

◆ The Golden Age Scholarship

This scholarship is granted to students who can contribute greatly and bring a hopeful future to the world.

◆ Success No.1
Buddha's Truth Afterschool Academy

Happy Science has over 180 classrooms throughout Japan and in several cities around the world that focus on afterschool education for children. The education focuses on faith and morals in addition to supporting children's school studies.

◆ Angel Plan V

For children under the age of kindergarten, Happy Science holds classes for nurturing healthy, positive, and creative boys and girls.

◆ Future Stars Training Department

The Future Stars Training Department was founded within the Happy Science Media Division with the goal of nurturing talented individuals to become successful in the performing arts and entertainment industry.

◆ New Star Production Co., Ltd.
ARI Production Co., Ltd.

We have companies to nurture actors and actresses, artists, and vocalists. They are also involved in film production.

DOCUMENTARY MOVIE
HEART TO HEART

In this documentary movie, Happy Science University students visit these NPO activities to discover what salvation truly is, and on the meaning of life, through heart-to-heart interviews.

ABOUT HAPPY SCIENCE MOVIES

THE REAL EXORCIST

New Movie Coming Early Summer 2020!

BEST FEATURE FILM
17th Angel Film Awards
2020
Monaco International Film Festival

BEST VISUAL EFFECTS
17th Angel Film Awards
2020
Monaco International Film Festival

BEST FEMALE ACTOR
17th Angel Film Awards
2020
Monaco International Film Festival

BEST FEMALE SUPPORTING ACTOR
17th Angel Film Awards
2020
Monaco International Film Festival

BEST FEATURE FILM
EKO International Film Festival
2020

BEST SUPPORTING ACTRESS
EKO International Film Festival
2020

IMMORTAL HERO

On VOD NOW

Story

Makoto Mioya, a highly successful Japanese author and publisher, has a life-threatening, near-death experience. Powerful spiritual beings with whom he has communicated most of his adult life visit Makoto to remind him he has the power within to heal himself. Reborn, Makoto commits his life to sharing the almighty wisdom he receives from the spiritual realm. As doubters, including some of his own family, challenge and question his newfound ardor, Makoto must find a way to connect with his family and the 'family of man' to inspire a better world.

36 Awards from 8 Countries!

SPAIN
BARCELONA INTERNATIONAL FILM FESTIVAL 2019
[THE CASTELL AWARDS]

SPAIN
MADRID INTERNATIONAL FILM FESTIVAL 2019
[BEST DIRECTOR OF A FOREIGN LANGUAGE FEATURE FILM]

ITALY
DIAMOND FILM AWARDS JUL 2019
[WINNER (NARRATIVE FEATUREFILM)]

ITALY
FLORENCE FILM AWARDS JUL 2019
[HONORABLE MENTION: FEATURE FILM]

USA
INDIE VISIONS FILM FESTIVAL JUL 2019 [WINNER (NARRATIVE FEATURE FILM)]

ITALY
FLORENCE FILM AWARDS JUL 2019
[BEST ORIGINAL SCREENPLAY]

...and more!

For more information, visit ***www.immortal-hero.com***

Lineup of Happy Science Movies

Discover the spiritual world you have never seen and come close to the Heart of God through these movies.

1994
+ **The Terrifying Revelations of Nostradamus**
(live action)

1997
+ **Love Blows Like the Wind**
(animation)

2000
+ **The Laws of the Sun**
(animation)

2003
+ **The Golden Laws**
(animation)

2006
+ **The Laws of Eternity**
(animation)

2009
+ **The Rebirth of Buddha**
(animation)

2012
+ **The Final Judgement**
(live action)

+ **The Mystical Laws**
(animation)

2015
+ **The Laws of the Universe - Part 0**
(animation)

2016
+ **I'm Fine, My Angel**
(live action)

2017
+ **The World We Live In**
(live action)

2018
+ **Heart to Heart**
(documentary)

+ **DAYBREAK**
(live action)

+ **The Laws of the Universe - Part I**
(animation)

2019
+ **The Last White Witch**
(live action)

+ **Life is Beautiful - Heart to Heart 2 -**
(documentary)

+ **Immortal Hero**
(live action)

- Coming Soon -

2020
+ **The Real Exorcist**
(live action)

+ **Kiseki to no Deai - Kokoro ni Yorisou 3 -**
(lit. Encounters with Miracles - Heart to Heart 3 -)
(documentary)

+ **Twiceborn**
(live action)

*Contact your nearest local branch for more information on how to watch HS movies.

CONTACT INFORMATION

Happy Science is a worldwide organization with faith centers around the globe. For a comprehensive list of centers, visit the worldwide directory at *happy-science.org*. The following are some of the many Happy Science locations:

UNITED STATES AND CANADA

New York
79 Franklin St., New York, NY 10013
Phone: 212-343-7972
Fax: 212-343-7973
Email: ny@happy-science.org
Website: happyscience-na.org

New Jersey
725 River Rd, #102B, Edgewater, NJ 07020
Phone: 201-313-0127
Fax: 201-313-0120
Email: nj@happy-science.org
Website: happyscience-na.org

Florida
5208 8th St., St. Zephyrhills, FL 33542
Phone: 813-715-0000
Fax: 813-715-0010
Email: florida@happy-science.org
Website: happyscience-na.org

Atlanta
1874 Piedmont Ave., NE Suite 360-C
Atlanta, GA 30324
Phone: 404-892-7770
Email: atlanta@happy-science.org
Website: happyscience-na.org

San Francisco
525 Clinton St.
Redwood City, CA 94062
Phone & Fax: 650-363-2777
Email: sf@happy-science.org
Website: happyscience-na.org

Los Angeles
1590 E. Del Mar Blvd., Pasadena, CA 91106
Phone: 626-395-7775
Fax: 626-395-7776
Email: la@happy-science.org
Website: happyscience-na.org

Orange County
10231 Slater Ave., #204
Fountain Valley, CA 92708
Phone: 714-745-1140
Email: oc@happy-science.org
Website: happyscience-na.org

San Diego
7841 Balboa Ave., Suite #202
San Diego, CA 92111
Phone: 619-381-7615
Fax: 626-395-7776
E-mail: sandiego@happy-science.org
Website: happyscience-na.org

Hawaii
Phone: 808-591-9772
Fax: 808-591-9776
Email: hi@happy-science.org
Website: happyscience-na.org

Kauai
3343 Kanakolu Street, Suite 5
Lihue, HI 96766, U.S.A.
Phone: 808-822-7007
Fax: 808-822-6007
Email: kauai-hi@happy-science.org
Website: kauai.happyscience-na.org

Toronto
845 The Queensway
Etobicoke ON M8Z 1N6 Canada
Phone: 1-416-901-3747
Email: toronto@happy-science.org
Website: happy-science.ca

Vancouver
#201-2607 East 49th Avenue
Vancouver, BC, V5S 1J9, Canada
Phone: 1-604-437-7735
Fax: 1-604-437-7764
Email: vancouver@happy-science.org
Website: happy-science.ca

INTERNATIONAL

Tokyo
1-6-7 Togoshi, Shinagawa
Tokyo, 142-0041 Japan
Phone: 81-3-6384-5770
Fax: 81-3-6384-5776
Email: tokyo@happy-science.org
Website: happy-science.org

Seoul
74, Sadang-ro 27-gil,
Dongjak-gu, Seoul, Korea
Phone: 82-2-3478-8777
Fax: 82-2-3478-9777
Email: korea@happy-science.org
Website: happyscience-korea.org

London
3 Margaret St.
London,W1W 8RE United Kingdom
Phone: 44-20-7323-9255
Fax: 44-20-7323-9344
Email: eu@happy-science.org
Website: happyscience-uk.org

Taipei
No. 89, Lane 155, Dunhua N. Road
Songshan District, Taipei City 105, Taiwan
Phone: 886-2-2719-9377
Fax: 886-2-2719-5570
Email: taiwan@happy-science.org
Website: happyscience-tw.org

Sydney
516 Pacific Hwy, Lane Cove North,
NSW 2066, Australia
Phone: 61-2-9411-2877
Fax: 61-2-9411-2822
Email: sydney@happy-science.org

Malaysia
No 22A, Block 2, Jalil Link Jalan Jalil Jaya 2,
Bukit Jalil 57000, Kuala Lumpur, Malaysia
Phone: 60-3-8998-7877
Fax: 60-3-8998-7977
Email: malaysia@happy-science.org
Website: happyscience.org.my

Brazil Headquarters
Rua Domingos de Morais 1154,
Vila Mariana, Sao Paulo SP
CEP 04009-002, Brazil
Phone: 55-11-5088-3800
Fax: 55-11-5088-3806
Email: sp@happy-science.org
Website: happyscience.com.br

Nepal
Kathmandu Metropolitan City Ward
No. 15,
Ring Road, Kimdol,
Sitapaila Kathmandu, Nepal
Phone: 97-714-272931
Email: nepal@happy-science.org

Jundiai
Rua Congo, 447, Jd. Bonfiglioli
Jundiai-CEP, 13207-340
Phone: 55-11-4587-5952
Email: jundiai@happy-science.org

Uganda
Plot 877 Rubaga Road, Kampala
P.O. Box 34130, Kampala, Uganda
Phone: 256-79-3238-002
Email: uganda@happy-science.org
Website: happyscience-uganda.org

HAPPINESS REALIZATION PARTY

The Happiness Realization Party (HRP) was founded in May 2009 by Master Ryuho Okawa as part of the Happy Science Group to offer concrete and proactive solutions to the current issues such as military threats from North Korea and China and the long-term economic recession. HRP aims to implement drastic reforms of the Japanese government, thereby bringing peace and prosperity to Japan. To accomplish this, HRP proposes two key policies:

1) Strengthening the national security and the Japan-U.S. alliance, which plays a vital role in the stability of Asia.

2) Improving the Japanese economy by implementing drastic tax cuts, taking monetary easing measures and creating new major industries.

HRP advocates that Japan should offer a model of a religious nation that allows diverse values and beliefs to coexist, and that contributes to global peace.

*For more information, visit **en.hr-party.jp***

ABOUT IRH PRESS

IRH Press Co., Ltd., based in Tokyo, was founded in 1987 as a publishing division of Happy Science. IRH Press publishes religious and spiritual books, journals, magazines and also operates broadcast and film production enterprises. For more information, visit *okawabooks.com*.

Follow us on:

Facebook: Okawa Books   **Twitter:** Okawa Books
Goodreads: Ryuho Okawa   **Instagram:** OkawaBooks
Pinterest: Okawa Books

RYUHO OKAWA'S LAWS SERIES

The Laws Series is an annual volume of books that are mainly comprised of Ryuho Okawa's lectures on various topics that highlight principles and guidelines for the activities of Happy Science every year. *The Laws of the Sun*, the first publication of the Laws Series, published in 1987. Since then, all of the Laws Series' titles have ranked in the annual best-selling list for more than two decades, setting sociocultural trends in Japan and around the world.

THE TRILOGY

The first three volumes of the Laws Series, *The Laws of the Sun*, *The Golden Laws*, and *The Nine Dimensions* make a trilogy that completes the basic framework of the teachings of God's Truths. *The Laws of the Sun* discusses the structure of God's Laws, *The Golden Laws* expounds on the doctrine of time, and *The Nine Dimensions* reveals the nature of space.

BOOKS BY RYUHO OKAWA

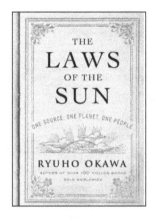

THE LAWS OF THE SUN
ONE SOURCE, ONE PLANET, ONE PEOPLE

Paperback • 288 pages • $15.95
ISBN: 978-1-942125-43-3

IMAGINE IF YOU COULD ASK GOD why He created this world and what spiritual laws He used to shape us—and everything around us. If we could understand His designs and intentions, we could discover what our goals in life should be and whether our actions move us closer to those goals or farther away.

At a young age, a spiritual calling prompted Ryuho Okawa to outline what he innately understood to be universal truths for all humankind. In *The Laws of the Sun*, Okawa outlines these laws of the universe and provides a road map for living one's life with greater purpose and meaning.

In this powerful book, Ryuho Okawa reveals the transcendent nature of consciousness and the secrets of our multidimensional universe and our place in it. By understanding the different stages of love and following the Buddhist Eightfold Path, he believes we can speed up our eternal process of development. *The Laws of the Sun* shows the way to realize true happiness—a happiness that continues from this world through the other.

---

*For a complete list of books, visit **okawabooks.com***

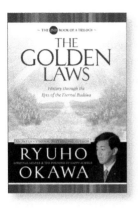

THE GOLDEN LAWS
HISTORY THROUGH THE EYES OF THE ETERNAL BUDDHA

Paperback • 201 pages • $14.95
ISBN: 978-1-941779-81-1

Throughout history, Great Guiding Spirits of Light have been present on Earth in both the East and the West at crucial points in human history to further our spiritual development. *The Golden Laws* reveals how Divine Plan has been unfolding on Earth, and outlines 5,000 years of the secret history of humankind. Once we understand the true course of history, through the past, the present and into the future, we cannot help but become aware of the significance of our spiritual mission in the present age.

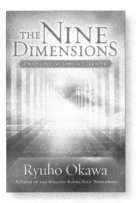

THE NINE DIMENSIONS
UNVEILING THE LAWS OF ETERNITY

Paperback • 168 pages • $15.95
ISBN: 978-0-982698-56-3

This book is a window into the mind of our loving God, who designed this world and the vast, wondrous world of our afterlife as a school with many levels through which our souls learn and grow. When the religions and cultures of the world discover the truth of their common spiritual origin, they will be inspired to accept their differences, come together under faith in God, and build an era of harmony and peaceful progress on Earth.

---

*For a complete list of books, visit **okawabooks.com***

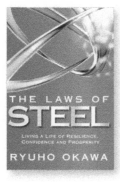

THE LAWS OF STEEL

LIVING A LIFE OF RESILIENCE, CONFIDENCE AND PROSPERITY

Paperback • 264 pages • $16.95
ISBN: 978-1-942125-65-5

This book is a compilation of six lectures that Ryuho Okawa gave in 2018 and 2019, each containing passionate messages for us to open a brighter future. This powerful and inspiring book will not only show us the ways to achieve true happiness and prosperity, but also the ways to solve many global issues we now face.

THE REASON WE ARE HERE

MAKE OUR POWERS TOGETHER TO REALIZE GOD'S JUSTICE -CHINA ISSUE, GLOBAL WARMING, AND LGBT-

Paperback • 215 pages • $14.95
ISBN: 978-1-943869-62-6

The Reason We Are Here is a book of thought that is unlike any other: its global perspective, timely opinion on current issues, and spiritual class are unmatched. The main content is the lecture in Toronto, Canada given in October 2019 by Ryuho Okawa.

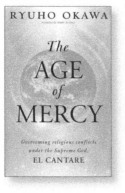

THE AGE OF MERCY

OVERCOMING RELIGIOUS CONFLICTS UNDER THE SUPREME GOD, EL CANTARE

Hardcover • 110 pages • $22.95
ISBN: 978-1-943869-51-0

Why are there conflicts in the world? How can people understand each other better? This book is a message from the Supreme God, who has been guiding humankind from the beginning of creation.

---

*For a complete list of books, visit **okawabooks.com***

LOVE FOR THE FUTURE
BUILDING ONE WORLD OF FREEDOM AND DEMOCRACY UNDER GOD'S TRUTH

Paperback • 312 pages • $15.95
ISBN: 978-1-942125-60-0

This is a compilation of select international lectures given by Ryuho Okawa during his (ongoing) global missionary tours. It espouses that freedom and democracy are vital principles to foster peace and shared prosperity, if adopted universally.

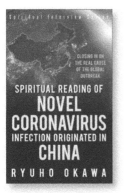

SPIRITUAL READING OF NOVEL CORONAVIRUS INFECTION ORIGINATED IN CHINA
CLOSING IN ON THE REAL CAUSE OF THE GLOBAL OUTBREAK

Paperback • 278 pages • $13.95
ISBN: 978-1-943869-77-0

This worldwide pandemic is not a mere act of nature nor a coincidence, but rather, heaven's warning to humanity, especially China. Through this book, you can find out "the immunity" against the novel coronavirus, among other shocking truths.

SPIRITUAL MESSAGES FROM OSCAR WILDE
LOVE, BEAUTY, AND LGBT

Paperback • 80 pages • $9.95
ISBN:978-1-943869-50-3

Why did Oscar Wilde write *the Happy Prince*?
The Astonishing Truth:
– His spiritual connection to Jesus Christ
– The deeper meaning behind his homosexuality
– Advice for the LGBT people to become happy

---

*For a complete list of books, visit **okawabooks.com***

THE NEW RESURRECTION
My Miraculous Story of Overcoming Illness and Death

THE ROYAL ROAD OF LIFE
Beginning Your Path of Inner Peace, Virtue, and a Life of Purpose

THE LAWS OF GREAT ENLIGHTENMENT
Always Walk with Buddha

I CAN
Discover Your Power Within

HONG KONG REVOLUTION
Spiritual Messages of the Guardian Spirits of Xi Jinping and
Agnes Chow Ting

THE STARTING POINT OF HAPPINESS
An Inspiring Guide to Positive Living with Faith, Love,
and Courage

HEALING FROM WITHIN
Life-Changing Keys to Calm, Spiritual, and Healthy Living

THE UNHAPPINESS SYNDROME
28 Habits of Unhappy People (and How to Change Them)

THINK BIG!
Be Positive and Be Brave to Achieve Your Dreams

---

*For a complete list of books, visit **okawabooks.com***

Lightning Source UK Ltd.
Milton Keynes UK
UKHW012022031120
372739UK00003B/45